AF496522

Art Education in a Postmodern World:
Collected Essays

Edited by Tom Hardy

Series editor: John Steers

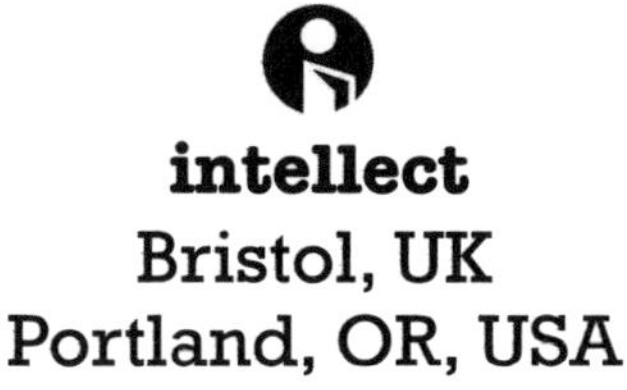

intellect
Bristol, UK
Portland, OR, USA

First Published in the UK in 2006 by
Intellect Books, PO Box 862, Bristol BS99 1DE, UK
First Published in the USA in 2006 by
Intellect Books, ISBS, 920 NE 58th Ave. Suite 300, Portland, Oregon 97213-3786, USA

A catalogue record for this book is available from the British Library

ISBN 1-84150-146-8
ISSN 1747-6208
Cover Design: Gabriel Solomons
Copy Editor: Holly Spradling

Printed and bound by The Cromwell Press, Trowbridge, Wiltshire

Contents

Acknowledgements

I am indebted to the contributors for their time and patience, revising and updating texts. I would particularly like to thank John Steers and Nick Stanley for their astute proof-reading and invaluable advice on the format of this collection. This book is dedicated to Rose, Olivia, Harriet and Beatrice; and to my students, past and present, whose work has been the proof of the pudding …

Tom Hardy

Preface

This book is the third in a planned series of anthologies dealing with a range of issues in art and design education. Titles published to date are *Critical Studies in Art & Design Education* and *Histories of Art and Design Education*. The primary – but not exclusive – source of chapters are papers previously published in the [International] Journal of Art & Design Education and where appropriate these have been updated. It should be noted that any references to the English National Curriculum statutory Orders, etc., are to that version of the curriculum current at the time of the original publication.

The National Society for Education in Art and Design is the leading national authority in the United Kingdom, combining professional association and trade union functions, which represents every facet of art, craft and design in education. Its authority is partly based upon a century-long concern for the subject, established contacts within government and local authority departments, and a breadth of membership drawn from every sector of education from the primary school to universities. More information is available at **www.nsead.org** or from NSEAD, The Gatehouse, Corsham Court, Corsham, Wiltshire SN13 0BZ (Tel: 01249 714825).

John Steers
Series editor

Introduction: Nailing Jelly: Art Education in a Postmodern world

Tom Hardy

We live in a postmodern age. The artistic and philosophical zeitgeist is one of a deconstructive challenge of absolutes, an abrogation of the tired conventions of modernism, a resistance to the exclusivity implied by long-held aesthetic principles, deliberate ambiguity and a mistrust of language. Thus, fuelled by dissenting views and contradictory by nature, definition of this condition would seem to be a tall order: akin to nailing jelly to the ceiling. Even so, it is a paradigm which has changed art and design, architecture, music and the theatre beyond recognition in the last two decades of the twentieth century.

It has given us the MI5 building at Vauxhall, sampling and rap in music, *Jerry Springer: the Opera*, Galliano and Brit art. It is strange, therefore, that so little has been written to try and corral the paradoxical concepts which shape and drive the contemporary art world for the consumption of teachers, trainee teachers and students in secondary and further education. I hope that, despite what Stuart MacDonald calls 'the promiscuity of the subject,' this collection will provide the uninitiated with a toehold.

What is postmodern art?
Ceçi n'est pas une pipe.

René Magritte's play with meaning (i.e. this is not a pipe, it is a painting) heralded the post-structural wrestle with linguistic reliability and, in turn, the postmodern quest by visual artists for interactive dialogue and playful ambiguity.

The term postmodernism first appeared in print in Joseph Hudnot's *Architecture and the Spirit of Man* (1949). It was originally used to mean simply 'after modernism' but, with the Hegelian inevitability that antithesis follows thesis, it has more recently come to mean 'against modernism'. However, adopting a constructive postmodern approach does not necessarily mean a rejection of all that the twentieth century had to offer, but an overlaying of a critical eye and language which challenges the conventions of modernism, while picking over its tastier morsels and revisiting all that modernism rejected. Charles Jencks, for one, viewed the postmodern 'as the preservation as well as the transformation of modernism.'[1]

It is true that, in some fields, a narrow reading has led to simplistic outcomes. In the field of contemporary pop music it seems merely to have led to the dead end of appropriation (sampling) without much in the way of innovation. However, in the visual arts, the tendency has not been to strip down but to add the dimensions of interaction and discourse. One has only to see the revival of naturalistic painting to know that traditional skills are not necessarily eschewed but given extra breadth and social relevance. If this were to be demonstrated with a Venn diagram, modernism might be seen to be the yolk in a postmodern fried egg.

Unlike the linear approach of modernism, the approach of postmodernism is multifaceted, and hence makes room for modernism.[2]

In a nutshell the principles, which have converged to underpin the movement, are as follows:

1. **The Little Narrative**. Individual stories and symbols but within the context of a cultural melting pot.

   ... in classes that are increasingly multicultural ... this means consideration of alternative points of view, with particular attention to minorities and gender issues.[3]

   This runs hand in hand with the push for citizenship in schools (and a more politicized youth in the wake of the anti-globalization movement and the war in Iraq), and in parallel with the massive recent expansion of personal web logs, home pages and all that the Internet has to offer in terms of interaction. The phrase 'interconnected differences'[4] has found some currency in debate on the subject.

   Here the trend of the artist as collaborator rather than solitary 'hero' or romantic outsider becomes apparent as feminist or minority cultural narratives are explored. Indeed, this respect for the group over the individual might be seen as reaction to the 'There is no such thing as society' pronouncements of the Thatcher era.

2. **Iconoclasm**. The value of artwork is explored and questioned and the accepted canon is balanced with a socio-political regard for the place of women and non-western practitioners in the history of art.

   The role of black culture in this period of reconfiguration has been to divest art of its current despair and create in its place a new optimism, an alternative worldview, and an unparalleled critical stance.[5]

   There is, though, a danger of undermining such hard-won respect when 'the nascent orthodoxies of PM [...] can only see the distinctive formal features of

Black expressive culture in terms of pastiche, quotation, parody and paraphrase,'[6] the main weapons in the postmodern armoury.

3. **Dialogue and Text**. The meaning of art is explored through deconstruction, discourse and the encouragement of multiple interpretations. Recently, Nicolas Serota, Director of the Tate Galleries, encapsulated the postmodern mindset when he remarked, 'There will not always be an answer to every question. Art obliges us to answer questions for ourselves.'[7] Symbolism has always been part of the artist's tool kit; it was inevitable that semiotics would play a part in a new movement.

4. **Eclecticism**. The deliberate plucking of elements out of their original contexts and bringing them together to form new aesthetic relationships and tensions are common postmodern traits. Jencks refers to this as 'Double Coding.'[8] Ambiguities and surprises, often with humour, are trademarks of 'pomo' and such playfulness contrasts with the 'po-faced' seriousness of the 'modernistas'.

A few jokes would help to open up the absurdity of the way things are.[9]

The thrust, therefore, of postmodernism is critique: an exposé of the myth of originality and the bias of the accepted historical narrative. Pluralism and difference replace the linear concept of coherent 'schools' or 'movements'. Conclusions are unlikely: all is deemed work in progress.

The debate

Critics have expressed concern that postmodernism rejects qualitative judgment and that we have entered a state of relativism where 'no works are more deserving or rewarding of attention than any other.'[10] This is, of course, not new. One only needs to recall the tabloid furore over pop art or Carl Andre's 'bricks'. Far more insidious is the patrician assumption that art should aspire to a Euro-centric template and that quality can be judged only by experts steeped in Gombrich and the meta-narratives (concerning meaning, truth and emancipation) of the Enlightenment.

Some fear the loss of an aesthetic sensibility in favour of pastiche and an 'anything goes' ethos if art, in the form of eclectic postmodernism, cuts itself adrift from history. But who is to say that a new aesthetic will not emerge from this eclecticism? History tells us that it always does. The cut and paste pan-cultural compositional style and the synaesthetic subject matter of the Beatles, while seeming ground-breaking to music aficionados of the 60s, has since been regarded as the apotheosis of aesthetic coherence for subsequent generations of songwriters.

In a curious way the postmodern artist, composer, and writer each has an openness to the cultural resources of past epochs and often appropriates motifs and inserts them into new works in order to comment on the deep and serious complexities of the contemporary world.[11]

Some have voiced the fear that art is becoming the servant of a socio-political agenda. This argument rather ignores the important place, in the history of art, of issue-inspired work and of the politically persuasive images of the likes of Gross, Dix, Picasso or Gericault. The debate about the worth of popular imagery is also somewhat stale having been done to death during pop art's heyday.

Indeed, we have been here many times before. In 1916 John Dewey called for an arts education that related to the world outside the school,[12] and in 1989 Jan Avgikos saw the emerging contemporary trend as revolutionary in the truest sense:

> *The schism that emerged in the polemic debates of the late 19th century between* l'art pour l'art *and politically engaged art remained as a deep underlying tension when Modernism, no longer satisfied with an art whose object is only itself, sought a resolution to its solipsistic conundrum. Fulfilling its need to determine its meaning by defining itself within the world, its theoretical object was found in paralleling systems of aesthetic production and consumption with a critique of social, political and economic systems.[13]*

Truly, the wheel has turned many times. The current trend for art which invites multiple interpretations and which responds with cynicism to modernity and corporate globalization finds resonance with the 'problem paintings' of the late nineteenth century. Indeed, those artists who provided a visual polemic to Ruskin's later social activism were reacting, with similar disillusionment, to the industrial revolution and all its concomitant injustices. In turn, we see echoes of Ruskin's and Morris's championing of the Gothic as an ideal.

> *Certain values emergent within postmodernism are reminiscent of values more typical of pre-than post- Renaissance Europe. Values that, today, would be called socialist or even Marxist were prominent through the middle ages but disappeared with the advent of the Renaissance.[14]*

Some feel that individual creativity is under threat. Exponents of postmodernism would point out that the cult of personality is a relatively recent phenomenon and might also cite the pre-Renaissance period as an ideal when craftsmen were anonymous and equal contributors to the artistic heritage of mankind. Television, the quintessential postmodern medium, is a group activity in much the same way as was the building of a Gothic cathedral.

Cubism's reaction to the emergence of photography at the turn of the twentieth century can be seen as a direct parallel to pomo's reaction to, and exploitation of, new media. With noteworthy symmetry, film itself has become a front line counter-insurgency medium in the protracted regime change.

Some have expressed concern that there is an emphasis on multiculturalism at the expense of the personally meaningful, but this is to assume that the two are mutually exclusive.

Michelle Kamhi argues that teachers "are easily seduced by urgent claims of the need to train students in 'visual literacy' to enable them to detect the powerful subliminal messages conveyed by popular and commercial culture."[15] But should visual acuity stop at the picture frame? As teachers, are we not educating for life as well as the gallery?

Some fear that we are in the throes of a reactionary backlash which calls for an end to experimentation. But close reading of Lyotard will flag the distinction between postmodernism in its many guises and this form of anti-modernism.

How can a postmodern perspective revitalize art teaching?

It seems to me that the naysayers miss the point. We live in exciting times.

I would suggest that, for a teacher, far from being a threat to cherished tradition, constructive, or 'affirmative', postmodernism could be the liberation of the subject and the herald of its integration into a whole school 'joined-up' curriculum celebrating as it does the interconnectedness of knowledge, learning experiences, international communities and life experience through the model of the artist as collaborator.

To divorce intellectual critical inquiry from the studio is to impoverish art practice.[16]

Postmodernism embraces new media and revels in literary sources. It celebrates difference but values inclusion and teamwork. Gone are the constraints of minimalism, thought by some to be the death throes of art; repealed is the prohibition of allegory, which, according to Craig Owens, has dominated fine art for some 200 years;[17] discredited is the isolationist intellectual snobbery of the 'Greenbergers' who relegated the crafts to a perceived second division; and dead as a dodo, the Lowenfeldian model of artist-as-teacher regurgitating the perennially accepted canon and passing on an exclusively personal aesthetic.

In their place, opportunities for Socratic dialogue, the rehabilitation of decoration and the integration of crafts, a renewal of figurative painting, and the proud appropriation of imagery and styles (particularly useful for the teaching of contextual studies as contemporary artists will wear their art (references) on their sleeves).

Indeed, recent research by the National Foundation for Educational Research convincingly concludes that schools which incorporate CAP (contemporary art practice) into their curriculum see an improvement in the motivation and enthusiasm of students while encouraging creativity and thinking skills and widening students' social and cultural knowledge. NFER'S Dick Downing elaborates: 'Young people are exposed to contemporary art practice all the time, for example through its influence on advertising, the internet and pop video; when it's included in the curriculum, CAP appears to provide a very accessible route to learning.'[19]

As educationalists, all should be grist to our mill. If you believe that an aesthetic sense is innate, instinctive, then no theoretical stance will stand in its way: quality will out. As Dennis Earl Fehr observes:

[Postmodern arts teachers] see their task as intermingling their knowledge with that of their students such that all parties arrive together at a new place.[20]

In short, the postmodern condition allows for the inclusion of discourse and the personal narratives of students. The 'co-constructivist'[21] concept of 'artist as collaborator' (with fellow students and teachers alike) paves the way for a curriculum that aspires to be more than the sum of the partners.

In spite of the publicity (mostly adverse) accorded to the ready-made outcomes of the more conceptual of the Young British Artists, I have never felt that discursive practice precludes traditional skills or aesthetic understanding, even if only employed ironically. On the contrary, it cries out for an eclectic approach to teaching which aims to broaden a student's skill base in the quest for the most effective method of prompting the desired debate/effect.

It encourages a creative integration of critical contextual studies rather than the oft-seen thoughtless regurgitation. It also assumes the artist's role within the community and the arts as central to a holistic curriculum. And, in a climate where the baccalaureate system is increasingly cited as the holy grail of cross-curricularity, the inclusive nature of the postmodern approach would seem to be timely, especially as a way for the visual arts to contribute significantly to 'Theory of Knowledge' requirements.

The broader debate regarding high and low art remains valid and healthy, but at school level the inclusion of popular imagery can be a gateway for students' appreciation of more classical forms. This debate, of course, has been raging in the English language arena for decades, where a study of *Eastenders* scripts always presupposed a relegation of Shakespeare. It never has; and neither will we see Gombrich or Greenberg sidelined, merely reassessed and absorbed in synthesis.

Conclusion

At present, exam specifications, imposed by successive governments for whom 'control' is a byword, require that secondary art students submit to reactionary precepts and an orthodoxy of process. There is also a tendency for teachers to play safe with exemplars from a traditionally accepted canon of artists and artworks. While we require that students contextualize their work within a contemporary value system that rejects such a notion of order, there would seem to be a difficult circle to square. And, of course, with the abandoning of a formalist approach, the corollary, which also needs to be addressed, is: how can the present obsolete foundations for assessment continue to hold sway?

This collection of writing will therefore not attempt to define a movement (for postmodernists, two's a crowd), but I hope that it might continue to inform debate and go some way to give a feel for common strands and a sample of concerns. While striving for praxis, I hope that this book might also help pave the way for further discussion at a policy-making level so that future specifications might allow for the true iconoclast and teaching methodologies unconstrained by anything but rigour and enthusiasm. The papers chosen are as follows:

A Manifesto for Art in Schools is John Swift and John Steers's influential benchmark proposal for a new approach to art teaching in a climate of philosophical change. Calling for a curriculum with an increased emphasis on 'difference, plurality and independence of mind', Swift and Steers map proposals for a divergent curriculum which gives space for risk-taking and 'testing provisional answers rather than seeking predetermined ones'.

In chapter 2, Nick Stanley documents a conversation with Sarat Maharaj about postmodern implications for the curriculum. Schools are described as post Gutenberg models of cultural eclecticism and, given this distinction, the discussion pursues why postmodern themes seldom appear at secondary level. They also yearn for a return to the pre-Thatcher concept of art school as 'critical shelter,' where 'failure' was seen as a positive route to fresh thinking.

Lee Emery's paper examines the ethical dilemma faced by teachers as to where to draw the line in an age when provocative art is geared more to afflict the comfortable than comfort the afflicted. The experiences of fifteen teachers from the UK and Australia are compared and she concludes that art teachers have a responsibility to provide a safe 'buffer zone' in the classroom for discussion of such imagery.

The segued papers of Stuart MacDonald echo the hope of a number of fellow contributors: that a postmodern condition might challenge the 'nationalisation of curricula,' but bemoans its limitations given the lack of 'models' or 'cogent ideas' where postmodernism is applied to art education. He calls for a 'grand dialogue' rather than a 'grand narrative', and suggests that contemporary contextual study remains the best tool for promoting a broad cultural literacy.

Burgess and Reay also sound a note of caution and challenge blind adherence to a postmodern agenda. Whilst admitting that recent turbulent times in education have resulted in a retreat to safe orthodoxies, and a retreat from feminist perspectives, they urge scepticism and warn that the postmodern paradigm might, when deconstructed, be a wolf in sheep's clothing, maintaining the status quo under a different guise.

John Danvers's paper discusses the holistic nature of knowledge, the convergent relationship between art and science, and the ways in which both spheres have moved from absolutism to 'contingency and relativity'.

Malcolm Miles's essay flags the value of 'critical distance', and argues the case for art as a continuous criticism of society, whilst mulling over the conundrum that art cannot 'represent suffering without aestheticising it'.

Paul Duncum's essay sets out the challenges facing art educators, particularly those steeped in the modernist tradition, in a Baudrillardian episteme. He argues for an art curriculum which encompasses broader aspects of visual culture, but which also explores the filters through which the media and political spin doctors present our world. In this he speculates that students are likely to be more savvy than their teachers when it comes to recognizing the significance of emerging cultural practices.

Robin Marriner's paper discusses post-structuralist implications for our concept of artwork as 'object of experience,' 'object of study' or 'object of knowledge', and the erosion of the perceived difference between high and low cultures.

Nicholas Addison's paper weighs the relative merits of quality and diversity suggesting that semiotic readings engage pupils on home ground, 'in the social, interactive potential of art'.

Dennis Atkinson's papers question the normative values embedded in the National Curriculum for Art, with reference to Foucault, Lacan and Derrida, and the concomitant obsolescence of current assessment specifications. He calls for a respect for, and recognition of, the legitimacy and coherence evident in local processes and traditions and for a more inclusive curriculum framework, driven by a respect for difference rather than an assessment structure 'grounded in a limited conception of practice': which, of course, brings us back to Swift and Steers …

Notes and References

1. Rose, M.A. [1991] *The Postmodern and the Post-industrial: A Critical Analysis*. Cambridge University Press.

2. Fehr, D. E. [1997] *Clutching the Lecturn or Shouting from the Back of the Hall?* Arts Education Policy Review 98, 4, pp. 27–31.

3. MacGregor, R. [1992] *Postmodernism, Art Educators, and Art Education*, Eric Digest.

4. www.magarstudiescenter.org/james.f.htm

5. Powell, R. [2002] *Black Art: a Cultural History*. Thames and Hudson, p. 167.

6. Jantjes, G. [1989] *A Fruitful Incoherence: Dialogues with Artists on Internationalism*. London: Institute of International Visual Arts, p. 163.

7. Serota, N. [2000] *'Who's Afraid of Modern Art?'* Richard Dimbleby Lecture.

8. Jencks C. [1991] 'Postmodern vs Late Modern' in I Hoesterey (ed.) *Zeitgeist in Babel: The Postmodernist Controversy*. Indiana University Press.

9. Hewison, R. [1990] *Future Tense – A New Art for the Nineties*. Methuen.

10. Marder Kamhi, M. *Where is the Art In Today's Education?* www.objectivistcenter.org/text/mkamhi-art-todays-art-education.asp

11. Efland A., Freedman K. and Stuhr p. [1996] *Postmodern Art Education: An Approach to Curriculum*. The National Art Education Association.

12. Dewey, J. [1916] *Democracy in Education*. New York, Macmillan.

13. Avgikos, J. [1989] *Anthropological War*. Artscribe, May.

14. Fehr, D. E. [1994] *Studies in Art Education* 35, 4.

15. Marder Kamhi, M. op. cit.

16. Sisson, E. "Circa 89" art education supplement, www.recirca.com/backissues/c89/supp-sisson.shtml

17. Owens, C. [1980] *The Allegorical Impulse: Towards A Theory Of Postmodernism*. October 12.

18. Sisson, E. "Circa 89" art education supplement, *Postmodernism, Art Educators, and Art Education*. Eric Digest. www.ericfacility.net/databases/ERIC_Digests/ed348328.html

19. Downing D. [2005] *School Art: What's in it?* A'N'D 14. NSEAD.

20. Fehr, D. [1997] op. cit.

21. Carnell, E. and Lodge, C. [2002] *Supporting Effective Learning*. London: Paul Chapman Publishing.

Chapter 1: A Manifesto for Art in Schools

John Swift & John Steers

This Manifesto proposes alternative ways of improving Art in Education. It is addressed to all who teach and learn art, who work in fields where art and education are important, and to administrators and policy makers in education, the arts and government.

Rationale and proposals for art
Preface
This manifesto bases its suggestions on a postmodern view of art in education with an emphasis on difference, plurality and independence of mind. The proposals derive from the rationale and argue for more decision-making and autonomy for teachers and learners within a climate that emphasises and expects enquiry, experiment and creative opportunity. For this to happen the subject matter of art, ways of approaching it, and improved means of encouraging diversity and innovation must be developed. This implies that the values within the current statutory Orders for Art, the initial education and in-service development of teachers, and the nature and purpose of assessment must be reconsidered. This manifesto addresses the areas that impinge on the activity of art in schools, makes critical comment on the effect of current ideology and practice, and provides a rationale and proposals for its implementation.

Rationale
The rationale is based on three fundamental principles: difference, plurality, and independent thought. Through their application in art practice and theory, knowledge and knowing will become understood as a negotiation of ideas which arise from asking pertinent questions, and testing provisional answers rather than seeking predetermined ones. The emphasis is on the learner and learning, negotiating what they learn, learning how to learn, and understanding knowledge as a multiplicity of changing hypotheses or theories which are subject to evidence, proof, argument and embodiment. As such *difference* becomes a locus for action and discussion at a personal and social level, *plurality* points to a variety of methods, means, solutions and awareness for any issue, and *independent thought* develops individuality, the capacity to challenge, and creativity through introspection into the nature of learning and teaching in art. These abilities are as vital for teachers as they are for learners.

The value of art education
Rationales are commonly understood as either intrinsic, i.e., for values only obtained through the study of art, or extrinsic, i.e., for values obtained across many

subjects and in which art plays a contributory role. In reality the two may be more intertwined than is generally acknowledged. For clarity of understanding, practice and theory are listed separately and then together – in reality, the two activities work together and are seen as symbiotic.

Practice develops the ability to use materials and techniques intelligently, imaginatively, sensuously and experimentally in order to respond to objects and ideas creatively through personally meaningful, communicable artefacts in school, later life or professionally.

Theory enables the use of ideas, images and text as means of interrogating received opinion in order to form knowledge and understanding based on an awareness of how art functions and is valued in different cultures, societies and times.

The combination of art theory and practice therefore serves to develop a sense of enquiry, an ability to take practical and intellectual risks, to be conscious of decision-making in a reflexive manner, to seek for and evaluate creative responses in self and others, to be able to articulate reasons for preference, qualitative judgments, or comparative aesthetic values, and engage with art and nature in the public world.

Art (and other subjects) serve to develop proactive, creative thought and action, sensitivity to difference of approach and outcome, e.g., gender, culture, ability, age, etc., a flexible understanding of changing values in different societies and periods, the ability to use a specialised vocabulary effectively within other forms of communication, a broad view of what constitutes culture, and pleasure and satisfaction in such forms of life.

In the broadest sense, art and other subjects, through an emphasis on difference, plurality and independence of mind develop wider individual and social advantages such as interpersonal tolerance, awareness and sensitivity, creative solutions for different situations, informed habits of matching evidence and deduction, the means to learn for oneself, and to apply considered values towards human culture and the natural environment.

Art also contributes to the development of key skills valued by employers. Improving one's own learning and performance, problem-finding and solving, working with others, standards of literacy, communication and using the new technologies for a variety of purposes are among the personal attributes that may be developed positively through good programmes of art education.

Proposals

Introduction

The proposals below are made within a framework that recognises the different and distinct values, kinds of knowledge and practices of 'arts' subjects. The proposals deal with Art only, which is not to deny that many of the ideas are common to the arts, (especially those of attitude, provision, and the relationships between theory and practice), but to recognise that they are also common to all aspects of learning. Therefore no claims are made for any grouping of arts subjects, although the proposals are not hostile to this as a strategy given that each subject is allocated sufficient guaranteed time. The proposals argue for the inclusion of art as a mandatory school subject for all pupils throughout their period of compulsory schooling (i.e. from age 5 to 16). This does not necessarily imply the need for detailed statutory Orders. In part the proposal is based on the necessity of such study in an increasingly visual world, and in part on the significant number of pupils who opt for art as an examination subject.

The proposals question the undue emphasis that has been placed on the 'Curriculum'. Thus the proposals below cover a wider range of the factors that can be used to improve all forms of education, viz., the teacher, the learner, the subject, and forms of assessment. Further, these are linked with initial teacher education and in-service opportunity in order to suggest that the four areas should gain a new and revivified attention both at the beginning and during a teacher's career.

Problems and proposals

The items are listed as follows: teacher, learner, subject, assessment, teacher training and development. The left-hand column identifies what is seen as problematic; the right-hand column offers solutions based on the rationale. Thus there is some reactive criticism but a much larger amount of proactive and constructive suggestion.

Teacher

Restricted scope of action	More autonomy in deciding and planning an art curriculum, recognising that a range of distinctive rationales may be appropriate.
Restricted skills and expertise	
Primary and generalist trained	More time for art study, but more importantly, a different approach to experiment, response, and contextualisation of art work.

Secondary and specialist trained	Teachers need to develop a clearer personal understanding of aims and objectives. Less school-based study and more study of innovative pedagogy, contemporary art forms and practices, theories of the social construction of the child, the teacher and schooling, and the history and philosophy of art education.
Orthodox art approaches	Less text books that offer 'easy' answers or recipes, which encourage reliance on the 'new academicism,' and more emphasis on confidence building and risk taking, i.e. experimental activities where the results and procedures are impossible to predict (especially in ITT and InSET). Teachers need innovative and imaginative approaches to art and design activities that stimulate their imagination and encourage such qualities as empathy, playfulness, surprise, ingenuity, curiosity and individuality. Teachers should be helped to enjoy the means of discovery and risk-taking inherent in experimental practice and thought.
Limited media and learning opportunities	Construct a variety of approaches where no single obvious route is evident by devising a range of ways of working across different media and types of learning.
Outcome or product-led work	Employ reflective means to enable the learner to understand the relation of theory and practice while engaged (predominantly) with either, i.e., to study themselves during the learning process, and to help learners to become conscious of their patterns and procedures for learning.
Standardised sets of criteria	To understand the different intentions and reasons of learners rather than superimposing a standardised response, e.g. based on 'the elements', 'perspective' or 'realism'.
Limited teaching approach	Welcome difference by acting as a role model – being open to experiment, change, challenge, and also being identified as a participating discoverer and learner.

Learner

Entitlement	All pupils, including the most able, should be entitled to study art throughout their period of compulsory schooling.

Limited ambition set by limited education Identification of the personal as a subject for art, and in the understanding of art.

Alienation from art Placing the personal within the social, historical and other contexts in such a way as to encourage enquiry and develop ideas of evidence and relevance for the learner.

Lack of theoretical and practical coherence Activities that heighten awareness of theory and practice in combination, and the tensions within and across them.

Orthodox approaches Challenge 'typical' responses with innovative ideas and example which show changes in perception, identity, cultural grouping, etc.

Insufficient learner autonomy Offer learners a real opportunity to question and influence their education by negotiation of a variety of approaches, e.g., with more or less emphasis on theory or practice according to need, age, development, ability, etc., in lessons that exercise choice by definition.

Lack of choice Variety of approaches within theory and practice and in their combination, e.g., variety of media and mixed media, cross-subject and combined subject learning opportunities, and offer real-life experiences, e.g., art work in the community, assessing the public's responses to art, using personal/family material, making and designing for actual needs, creating desk-top publications of school art, etc.

Subject

Hierarchically ordered on received opinion Open up all cultural forms for interrogation, appraisal and evaluation – debate rather than state ideas of superior/inferior, rich/thin, complex/simple, fine/popular, etc.

Limited in medium and type Plan for a variety of alternative approaches by offering a broader selection to choose from, e.g., Media-based: drawing, painting, crafting, media studies, information technology, cross-disciplinary, multi-media, etc.
Type-based: Critical Studies, public art, community art, issues based, environmental or ecological art, etc.

<table>
<tr><td>Over historic/
academic</td><td>Address contemporary issues, current debates and practices through books, new technologies, slides, gallery visits and residency schemes. Examine art's changing role in different societies – how similar issues were dealt with and different ones recognised or not.
Study how art produced both within and without the UK affects our view of ourselves as individuals, groups and in terms of national identity.</td></tr>
<tr><td>Critical Studies
unambitious</td><td>Develop a clear rationale for its inclusion based on cultural transmission, real critical thought and reaction, and articulat debates, try role-play, and avoid 'unproblematic' pastiches of style.</td></tr>
<tr><td>One curriculum
restricts choice</td><td>Develop 'multiple visions' of the curriculum – a series of curricula with identifiable differences, e.g., of approach, content, medium or type, and/or a series of shorter curricula which could be built up as learning modules. For these to work effectively the means of assessment and criteria would also have to change.</td></tr>
</table>

Assessment

<table>
<tr><td>Criterion and norm
referencing</td><td>Develop a range and variety of assessment for clearly identified different purposes. Although individual assessment may be based on comparison with other individuals or groups, it should not be dependent on comparative means alone. Such an approach inhibits the ability to respond to change or difference. The learner's intention should be crucial to the way the teacher 'reads' the work.

Avoid 'invisible' criteria preferences such as 'accuracy', 'likeness', 'in perspective', 'expressive', unless they are clearly stated and explained in their various meanings.

Acknowledge hidden agenda; make them explicit and open to debate as opposed to being 'givens'.</td></tr>
<tr><td>Standardisation</td><td>Standardised outcomes make individual evaluation less relevant. Increased standardisation, for example, through the development of subject cores for GCSE and GCE 'A' level, is leading to a decrease in variety of these examinations and an increasing tendency to standardised responses.</td></tr>
</table>

Methods of assessment	Assessment that matters to the learner relates to intention, is Normative, and at best, self-generated. It enables knowledge of 'errors' and how to amend them. More consideration should be given to self-assessment and self-evaluation – self-awareness and judgment are very valuable life skills.
	Assessment should be authentic, i.e., reject testing in favour of procedures which require students to engage in long-term, complex, and challenging projects reflecting real-life situations. Data collected for analysis include portfolio evidence of developmental work, written or recorded (student reflections), and teacher-student dialogue.
Notions of objective judgment	Objectivity in art judgments is based on the amount of comparative, experiential knowledge we possess and can apply – as such, differences of opinion are to be expected and welcomed in making judgments.
Restricted preferences	Design broader-based expectations that reward experiment, challenge, and independent thinking and making, discourage safe 'reading between the lines', and place more emphasis on evaluation of portfolios and work during the learning process by examination boards, schools and teachers.

Teacher training and development

Initial Teacher (Training) Education	Consider the education of teachers not their ability to be trained.
Generalists are ill-equipped to teach, respond and mentor	Substantially increase time to allow for a change of approach with more emphasis on experimental making, evaluation of ones own working processes, awareness of contexts, and verbal sophistication in description, metaphor, and judgment. Specific subject knowledge is axiomatic if a teacher is to act as an effective subject mentor.
	Make more time to study and theorise a variety of different teaching styles and rationales and when and how to apply theirs effectively.
Specialists possess too little theoretical knowledge	Rethink the relationship between all higher education institutions and schools to better use the skills of both. There is a need for specialist art teachers at Key Stage 2.

<table>
<tr><td>In-service Education and Training</td><td>Establish a richer variety that is financially supported and allow teachers to select from, e.g., pedagogy, subject practice, subject theory, management, etc.</td></tr>
<tr><td>Opportunity</td><td>Vastly improve short, middle and long course availability both for and and not for qualification. Improve opportunities for partnerships, distance learning, and other means to counter-act limitations of opportunity. Recognise the contribution of a range of agencies including the key role of professional associations.</td></tr>
<tr><td>Quality</td><td>Require a defined amount of funded InSET on a frequent basis within a specified time as a necessary basis for continued qualified teaching status.</td></tr>
</table>

Conclusions

Merely modifying or replacing the curriculum Orders or national guidelines for Art will not in itself resolve the problems identified. The points above indicate the interconnectedness of teaching, learning, subject knowledge, assessment, and the preparation and development of teachers. All these factors need addressing if education (and within it art education) is to become a more meaningful and high quality experience for teachers and learners, and create the artists, craftspeople, designers and discerning consumers of art and design that Britain needs. The essential points of difference, plurality and independence of mind call for a refocusing in all areas:

1. Redesign the preparation and development of teachers in order to give them the confidence and ability to embody and promote risk-taking, personal enquiry, and creative action and thought both before and during their teaching career.

2. Open more opportunities for learners to understand art as something that does actually matter in their lives and has relevance to present and future action. Offer more choice, autonomy and empowerment though the development of a more critical, enquiring reflexive and creative mindset, and to assist self-generated and self-aware learning.

3. Broaden the range of choice and type of study available across all forms of art without any implied hierarchy. Offer opportunity for different types of study and a range of media planned to raise consciousness of current personal and social issues, their representation in past and present art forms, and through different cultures. This requires the development of a diversity of curricula where the various aims, practices and purposes would be designed to raise difference, plurality and independence through either modules related to age, ability or intention, or through specific approaches to areas of study, or a mixture of both.

4. Reconsider the values implicit in current evaluation, assessment and examination practices, to whom the results of such practices are addressed and for what purpose, and their respective usefulness.

In sum, the proposals call for more decision making and authority for teachers and learners within a climate of enquiry, risk-taking and creative opportunity. This means re-addressing the contents of art education, different approaches to it, and finding improved ways of encouraging diversity and innovation made evident through difference, plurality and independent thought. To develop these ideas in schools, we call for greater flexibility than allowed by the present statutory Orders. Investment is needed in innovative and creative curriculum development that seeks to develop rigorous new approaches and effective teaching and learning strategies. Reconsideration is needed of the education and development of teachers to provide the essential theoretical and philosophical underpinning needed to sustain them in practice. Reappraisal is needed of all forms of assessment and evaluation, including teacher appraisal, with probable profound implications for Government and its various education agencies throughout the United Kingdom, the examination boards and validating bodies. Only then will the fundamental values of art have a realistic opportunity to integrate with the current and future interests of learners and of society in ways that are meaningful for both the subject and the individual.

Note: Throughout this paper 'Art' as a school subject should be understood as referring to Art, Craft and Design.

Originally published in the *Journal of Art & Design Education*, volume 18 (1) 1999.

Chapter 2: Nick Stanley and Sarat Maharaj: A Discussion

Sarat Maharaj

NS

I wondered, Sarat, if I might bring together strands from our previous conferences.[1] Can we inter-relate secondary and tertiary education with some of the key terms developed in your paper.[2] You speak through James Joyce and Marcel Duchamp about theory/practice as a single area; about 'pure observation and direct experience' as notions to tussle with; about multiculturalism, cultural diversity and difference; about the end of the art school as 'critical shelter'; about performance, production and perfection overshadowing open-ended play and about the potential of anti-systemic thinking against the octopus managerialism of the mega-visual system.[3] Such postmodern themes seldom appear in secondary education. I think they should but could we ever entertain them there?

SM

At first sight, such ideas might seem rather abstract and hair-raisingly alien to the secondary school space. It would be a bit surprising if 'postmodernism' did get a look in as a word let alone crop up explicitly as a subject in the syllabus or whatever – as opposed to the post-secondary domain where it reigns as the ubiquitous, privileged object of study and instrument of analysis and critical commentary.

But this shouldn't obscure the fact that in the secondary school space some of the most intense-intimate experiences of the postmodern are played out in the schooling and shaping of the sense faculties. The school's acoustic environment is made up of a massively 'plugged-in' generation with its everyday gear of walkmans, earphones, TVs, personal stereos and CDs, cassette players, discmans, mobiles, calculators, Nintendo gameboys. It mirrors the hi-tech postmodern sound world – the post-post Gutenberg – where everything is mediated through some apparatus that stretches out the senses providing them with a back-up service. Voice and vocal vibration waves, sound and noise are related through some techno-medium – rendered as mixed, synthesised, sampled, hybridised sound stuff – questioning notions of the 'pure, natural senses and sound.' The school space is a criss-crossing and collaging of sound textures and tonalities, canonical and colloquial voice scripts. Sonic stuff from diverse continents collide and coalesce into rap, bhangra, pop, bollywood, techno. I guess even the sonic texture of Morris dancing is not untouched by this mediation and transfusion.

Schooling today takes place through an inescapable immersion in an assemblage of intensive – extensive sonic constructions which is linked with hi-speed image circulation – ads, film, TV and fashion fabrications and fictions of the mega-visual system. The local school whether in hard-urban Brixton or Wiltshire interacts with a swirling global media force – a telescoping of image-sound terrains and temporalities we associate with postmodernity. At post-secondary level it might just still be possible to feel that we can keep 'the postmodern' at bay by treating it as an academic topic amongst others. But in the powerful, emerging secondary school sound-image-word space – a schooling of the sense organs and body by saturation in the post-post Gutenberg – the art teacher, practitioner, educationist is pressed to ask how to engage critical awareness and activity.

NS

I had really not thought of the secondary area as so implicated in post-modern developments. Does that put it potentially in the same difficulty you describe for tertiary education when you speak of the failure of the art school as 'critical shelter'?

SM

By the late 1980s the art school came to be shaped by ideologies of professional delivery: success in market terms, art as career, instant visibility, art theory and criticism as promotional and marketing blurb, managerial speak, artistic monetarism. This was one side of the response to Thatcherite pressures to get art education in line with productivity and usefulness. But the period also saw vibrant, questioning, critical theory enter the curriculum – which perhaps has ended up by the 1990s as the institutional norm and part of the pressure to make art practice/theory a systematic, academically recognisable discipline like others. This signals the closure of 'critical shelter' – of the resistant vagaries of art practice itself as the educational model of experiment, exploration, open-ended process rather than the business of shifting art products. By the late 1990s, however, the production line of the Thatcherite art school is coming under fire from a new generation. Perhaps, if 'critical shelter' is to be used in 2000 it has to be defined and coined afresh for quite different circumstances.

NS

Can you elaborate?

SM

I suppose I'm looking at the double movement in the postmodern: on the one hand, image-sound-words are stripped bare of the sense of authenticity and authority that came from the aura of belonging 'essentially' to a particular culture, a singular history, an individual expression. As the aura of original location evaporates they become see-through signs in extra-rapid circulation mixing to produce new, hybrid constructions. But as the idea of cultures as discrete, fixed, separate entities and identities gives way to transfusions, cross-overs and swaps we should not forget that the machinery of hi-speed transmission also flattens out differences into an echoless one-dimensionality, the MacDonald's effect. 'Critical shelter' has to be defined between these two drives. As an antisystemic, rhizomatic mode of thinking it goes against the grain of the standardising drive. Can we imagine a practice centered on the anti-systemic? How do you translate it into an actual project in the Clapham classroom a teacher might ask?

NS

Absolutely, Sarat, what could one come up with?

SM

In any proposal we would have to be aware of Brixton and Wiltshire as distinct locales but also as located in a shared media-techno-space – an interpenetrating of locations. The project is itself a self-raising, self-erasing model. It's not a ready-made, off-the-shelf programme. It constructs its principles in the process of elaborating itself. I imagine about 20 students doing a driftwork – video, photo-sound recordings of passages and pathways through the school, leisure, sport, public spaces. This is a log book or journal made up of writing, found objects, drawings, photos, litter, sounds-scraps, film excerpts. The drift is an encounter with difference, the multicultural, otherness. It echoes elements of the late 1950s Situationist *dérive* and *détournement* – sharp twists of expectation in visits to immigrant clubs – watering holes and dives for 'outsiders' from Antilles, Martinique, North Africa. Situationist raids on 'otherness' were tinged with the desire to soak up exotic sensations, tastes, images, sounds and smells. But they were amongst the first practitioners to note and negotiate 'immigrant difference' against a growing sense of numbing, post-war consumerist sameness.

The Clapham drift seeks to write the familiar as the foreign – a *xeno-writing* or writing of the self as the outside and other – an autrebiography. It thinks through the historical limits of the Situationists by scanning its own strategies of recording and voicing contemporary otherness – everyday street life, menus, movement, food, dress, sounds, smells and sensations. It acts out and embodies ideas through sound-body movement – the discursive and performative are played off against each other. What emerges is a gear-changing *xeno-writing* – an idea, image, touch, taste, smell, sound writing activating body and senses. The model is about experiencing otherness, testing and trying out options, commenting and discussing, going down dead ends, backing out, rephrasing. It has neither a grandly universalist sweep nor is it entirely parish pump – it's a one-off thing that rubs the slate clean and dissolves itself each time in its own unfolding.

NS

You've grappled with these issues in practical ways with your class at Goldsmiths'
College. Does the 'self-erasing' model connect with your reference to the Beckett
quote – 'if you should fail, try hard again, fail better next time' – to the notion not
of polished and perfected production but making a principle of not succeeding? Is
it an intrinsic element of the postmodern project?

SM

In the high-visibility stakes much seems to depend on not putting a foot wrong and
on treating mistakes or failure as a terrible set-back. In turning the earnest, scout's
maxim upside down, the Beckett quote serves not so much as a counter principle
as an invitation to explore beyond the success mentality which grips the art school
today – a punishing, distorting attitude. Some failures, as E. M. Forster put it, are
really successes because they involve learning and thinking afresh rather than
simply smooth delivery. For Adorno, identity-thinking – practice that seeks success
by becoming one with what has been identified in advance as correct and right –
runs over otherness and difference like a steamroller. It fails to grapple with them
in their own terms. Non-identity thinking is about missing the target, probing the
gap between aim and what falls short of it, by working through random elements
and accidents along the way.

In *Two or Three Things I Imagine About Them* [Whitechapel, 1992] Alfredo Jaar and
Gayatri Spivak roved through the local Bangladeshi community – cafes, restaurants,
factories, shops – a multi-layered immigrant location that has seen Huguenots,
Jews, Pakistanis and Bangladeshis through to Somalian, Bosnian and Albanian
refugees of today. A promising match of theory, practice and consultation – but
members of the community walked into the gallery to ask that representations of
them be removed. A tendency to clam up about the event followed, to hush it up
perhaps to avoid tabloid ridicule. But, as Spivak stressed to me, a full airing of what
went wrong was essential. The idea of the show as successful delivery of a product
is at odds with it as trial and test, as open-ended experiment with cultural diversity
which is the spirit of the Beckett failure model for the Clapham school.

NS

I am reminded of some examples – *Woven Air* [Whitechapel] and its mish-mash of
approaches which might have been deemed a failure. But it served to stimulate
critique and counter-critique about representing other cultures and other
artisanal, non-fine art practices. Anthony Hockey's work in West Kerry portrayed
some villagers in the 1930s worse for booze but still at it at 3.00 am. The
uncompromising, rough-edged picture of the community was accepted. Much later
he was asked if he would remove some of the more 'unflattering' images. Does a
third example – Rachel Whiteread's Holocaust monument project for Vienna – link
up with your gloss on test and experiment opened up by 'failing better'?

SM

The claim of survivors and descendants that their 'sense of direct connection with the Holocaust' meant that they alone were able authentically to speak/not speak the immensity of the annihilation has to be respected. Such a claim should not, however, let others off the hook – those who might shrug off the Holocaust as having 'no direct connection' with them and therefore of no concern to them. Whiteread speaks of making the monument maquette as a process of learning about the Holocaust. The dilemmas over her project highlight the impossibility of 'direct experience' of an event as the sole criterion for involvement. We link up with events such as the Troubles in Northern Ireland, genocide in Bosnia and Rwanda, the Cambodian Year Zero, famine and starvation through the media techno-system. The seamless reportage-dissemination mechanism positions us as viewer-participants: we are both at one stage removed from and intimately in the carnage while watching far away events as if they were an on-going soap screened in our homes. This sense of the unreal real is a reason for Jean Baudrillard's somewhat provocative remark that 'the Gulf War did not happen' – dramatising complicities and convolutions that blur hard and fast distinctions between 'direct, secondhand and simulated experience.'

Someone in Derry or Belfast voices the Troubles from their particular location in Northern Ireland. It is both at one with and at odds with our screened and highly-constructed reception of the conflict in England – however much supplemented by our own 'direct experience' of IRA bombs. The lines of connection and complicity are more tangled than admitted by absolutist binaries such as authentic/ersatz, inside/outside. The Clapham project cannot shrug off the Troubles as none of our business because it's 'outside our direct experience.' Our immersion in the post-post-Gutenberg implicates us in its ethical tussles which stare us in the face even when we turn a blind eye to it.

NS

Your example is striking and interesting. We are often irritated in England that our European neighbours or 'international observers' can breeze into Northern Ireland to write it up in what we tend to assume to be naive, shallow, stereotypical. They are seen as messing about in somebody else's affairs. Yet one cannot help feeling that an 'insider's' ear for the language that differentiates the people of the place marking out cultural, social and political barriers and divisions – would be lost on an 'outsider.' Despite that, it's possible that the 'outsider' sees dimensions of the conflict 'insiders' cannot articulate. It seems it is this inside/outside opposition that is itself complex, inverted and turned inside out in the postmodern – presenting new responsibilities on the educational front.

SM

Does this perhaps become a little more clear in looking at certain extreme situations? The Truth and Reconciliation Commission in South Africa – perhaps not unlike some future post-ceasefire commission in Northern Ireland – has operated in a legalistic, if not strictly juridical, framework to extract accounts of the Apartheid machine's violations. But it has been obliged to step beyond its legalistic-linguistic limits to enact the search for forgiveness, reconciliation and post-apartheid openness by staging encounters between perpetrators and victims. Tears, eyeballing, gestures, weeping, paroxysms, touching – the striking resort to a performative mode is moving. For Adorno too the legalistic-linguistic fell short of the capacity to articulate what he called post-Auschwitz notes for a 'damaged life.' Perhaps Willie Docherty's videos of shadowy, half lit streets of Derry, mundane yet electric with menace, already prefigure the attempt to articulate something of the unrepresentable.

The Clapham project would have to mobilise a not dissimilar performative play against the limits of the discursive – to voice by means of a somatic-object language the difference and otherness that cannot be represented. Against the concern in identity-thinking and identity politics with shoring up fixed, pre-fashioned notions of self and other – seen as tribal absolutes and fundamentals – the Clapham driftwork's connective and conductive encounters with otherness evokes identity as liquid difference, as fluid in-betweeness. But beyond the ethical and multicultural dimensions of such a project, what of its more strictly visual elements? By using the modalities of photography, drawing, video, digital imaging, text, actual objects and film clips it seeks to cultivate a visual fluency that matches the street smart visuality of the postmodern everyday with its ads, consumerist imagery, styled commodities, malls, leisure spaces and supermarket vistas. Can a visual art project both take part in this street smart visuality – drawing on the post-post Gutenberg generation's remarkably sophisticated ability to read and decode its visual surroundings – and stand back from it for critical scrutiny? The tendency in traditional art historical and visual culture studies has been to want to translate commentary on visual experience into verbal, textual products. Can we get away from this received hierarchy in which the verbal is always top of the pack? The Clapham dérive chafes against the limits of the discursive: it tinkers with a visual lingo managing to swim in and out of street smart visuality unpicking it in terms of its own non-linguistic gear. Our explorations at Goldsmiths' are towards the *xeno-writing* of such a visual lingo.

Notes and References

1. The Art Curriculum in the Post Modern World, National Society of Education in Art & Design, in Birmingham, Bristol, Liverpool and Glasgow, 1997–98.

2. Paper to the Birmingham session of The Art Curriculum in the Postmodern World, National Society for Education in Art & Design, 17 September, 1997.

3. Archeologies of the Art School: Sarat Maharaj, Hans Ulrich Obrist and Gillian Wearing in New *Contemporaries*, Cornerhouse Manchester, Camden Arts Centre, CCA Glasgow, pp. 21–42.

Originally published in the *Journal of Art & Design Education*, volume 18 (1) 1999.

Chapter 3: Censorship in Contemporary Art Education

Lee Emery

Overview

This paper explores one of the complex issues that arise when students study contemporary art in the senior secondary school. The study draws upon interviews with fifteen secondary art teachers in Australia and England and focuses on the selection and censorship of artists and art works for student study. Given that cutting edge art must shock if it is to change artistic sensibility it would seem that the study of contemporary art must present students and teachers with many ethical dilemmas. The violent, sexually explicit, disgusting and psychologically disturbing, nature of many contemporary arts works make them potentially offensive, disturbing, provocative and confusing to young impressionable minds. While wishing to be open-minded and to teach inclusive curricula, art teachers are also aware of their accountability in the community and their responsibility for the well-being of their students. The study examines ways in which art teachers achieve *postmodernist* plurality in their programmes yet also respectfully stay within the parameters of the *modernist* school charter which defines certain limits within schooling systems.

Introduction

> *In a world which takes us ever further from our animal origins, art reminds us who we really are; human, animal, mortal. If today's art is disgusting it's only because life can be too.*[1]

The latest wave of contemporary artists, especially the Young British Artists (YBAs) of *Sensations*[2] fame, repeatedly turn to obscenity and unpleasant imagery as the substance of their art. So unpleasant is their art that in 1999 it was deemed far too contentious and confronting for Australian eyes. In deciding not to bring the *Sensations* exhibition to Australia the National Gallery of Australia deprived the Australian public of the critical debate and, some would say, 'media circus,' which surely accompanies such an exhibition. And, in denying Australians the chance to make up their own minds, Australian art students also missed the opportunity to see a collection of works which might have fuelled vigorous debate about the very nature and purposes of art itself. The censorship of such an exhibition from Australian eyes raises many issues for art education in the democratic world (and indeed in the undemocratic world!). Why is it that such an exhibition is censored? Who might find it offensive? Should art galleries only display uncontentious art works? Should people be protected from contentious art? And more importantly who decides what is contentious? This paper does not attempt to define what may be meant by contentious or 'disgusting' art but in general I am referring to recent art that is seen by many as shocking, obscene and/or psychologically disturbing. Some of these art works include excrement, garbage, video sequences of violence, mutated bodies, graphically violent scenes of brutality and may contain reference to things like child abuse, disease, medicine and death, shelter, exposure etc. I am not really referring to images which contain humour, although some fairly 'disgusting' works can contain wonderful irony and great humour while reviling at the same time!

This paper is part of a broader study involving interviews with ten secondary art teachers from Australia and five from England. The wider study was designed to find out how teachers introduced contemporary art in the senior curriculum. Of the Australian teachers three taught in private schools, two in Catholic schools and three in state maintained schools. The five English teachers taught in state maintained schools in (or near) London. One of the questions I asked teachers was how they selected artists for study and whether they censored any art works. In particular, I wanted to know whether controversial artists (known for their 'disgusting' works) were included. I also wanted to know whether art teachers adopted a form of 'house style' to curriculum development. In other words I wondered whether particular schools studied particular artists and whether students were actually discouraged from studying artists whose works were considered (by teachers, principals and parents etc.) to be 'distasteful,' obscene or simply 'disgusting.'

Most senior art curricula require students to study the works of contemporary artists but it is usually left to art teachers and students to select the artists to be studied. My regular visits to schools had shown that there are some artists who are extremely popular with both students and teachers and these artists are often the stimulus for students' own research projects and their own art work. Frida Kahlo, Andy Goldsworthy and Cindy Sherman, for example, seem to me to be frequently studied, while Andres Serrano, Damian Hirst and Sarah Lucas seem to be avoided. I was curious to know whether this perception was wrong or whether, if the latter artists were studied, how they were studied. How do teachers discuss unmade bed installations by Tracey Emin? What approaches to discussion do teachers use when students are introduced to Damian Hirst's dissected animal pieces? Do art teachers deal with the difficult social, cultural or political issues these artists explore? Furthermore which works by which artists are studied? How do art teachers deal with the dark side of Sherman's work as described in the following account?

After inventing media like images of 'beautiful' women, Sherman turned against 'beauty' with a ferocity rarely found in the history of art. In 1985 she substituted for her self-image a hideous melange of dolls, teddy bears, and toy monsters submerged in a stew of slime, vomit, pus, and glop that look as if they had oozed out of horror movies … Sherman's repellent and depressing pictures exemplify the 'abject' in life and art, that which is cast off, dirty, degraded, grotesque, and pathetic.[3]

Diverse classrooms

We all construct our own definition of 'disgusting' and what may be disgusting or offensive to one individual or group, may be quite acceptable to others. The one art work can trigger diverse responses and it is sometimes surprising to find out who is disgusted by what. In the 1970s when the Australian artist Ivan Durrant first placed a slaughtered cow in front of the National Gallery of Victoria, it wasn't the Hindu community or even vegetarians that reacted with disgust and horror, it was the thousands of barbecue-loving, steak-eating carnivores in the general population! Most failed to see that Durrant's cow piece was directed at them: a blatant statement about the hypocrisy of a society which voraciously eats hamburgers and steaks but finds it disgusting to think about or see animal slaughter. Some would remember Durrant's dinner parties at which surprised guests witnessed the butchering of live pigeons at the dinner table! In the 1970s this was regarded as shocking (although Durrant's events certainly did create a cult following in the Melbourne art community). Durrant's very realistic butcher's shop window, later displayed in the National Gallery of Victoria, subsequently inspired students to engage in lengthy discussion about animal liberation, food packaging, hamburger chains, battery hens, consumer cultures, cultural differences in eating habits, hunger etc. For some, the butcher's shop was seen as a symbol of the disgusting meat-eating habits of Australians generally, but for others the butcher's shop seemed no different to the one in their local shopping centre.

We all respond to controversial art works in different ways and art teachers are aware that within any one class students at differing levels of maturity and from different cultural and religious backgrounds will be offended by different things. Knowing this makes curriculum selection even more difficult because in trying to be 'politically correct' in relation to every issue (including age, religion, class, gender, culture etc.) the art teacher is left without any clear guidelines as to the way to proceed. Someone, it seems, is bound to be offended, no matter what is selected for study in the art curriculum. 'Disgusting' art presents the art teacher with complex ethical and aesthetic concerns. If art teachers include contentious works for study they run the risk of upsetting parents, principals and the community. However, if art teachers deliberately avoid controversial art works, teaching programmes fail to reflect the real-life issues that are the substance of much contemporary art today. Finding a satisfactory resolution between these two aspects involves critical sensitivity. Developing teaching programmes which tackle key issues, yet which also respectfully avoid offending students and the community can be similar to walking on egg shells; one proceeds with utmost caution.

Shock and disgust

There is something about disgusting art which attracts students and adults alike; fascinated as we all are by the rebellious, raw and subversive nature of it. I first saw Francesco Goya's image of *Saturn Devouring One of His Children* (1820–1823) when I was a secondary student. It was such a repulsive and obscene image that to this day, it epitomises the most depraved thing I can imagine. However, I was also curious about the mind of a person who could envisage such a thing. It seems that horror both fascinates and repels at the same time. We want to see, yet don't want to see. Art is a peep show on life and in the comfort of a gallery we can safely peek at aspects of humanity which we might never actually experience. Art galleries are full of disgusting images; rape scenes, wars, beheadings, martyrdoms etc. People are drawn to disgusting art work and many contemporary artists seek to explore those aspects of life which we normally choose to ignore. However, we do become desensitised to shock, and images which initially revile us, can in time become accepted and even common place. The crucifixion, for example, is a shocking image, yet its familiarity and iconic status in the Christian world mask its ghastliness. The 'public at large' does not object to crucifixion images being shown in galleries or even churches. However, it does object to new images in which elephant dung is placed on a Madonna figure (Chris Ofili) and it does object to an image of Christ on which the artist has urinated (Andres Serrano). The juxtaposition of religious figures with bodily excretions is seen as offensive to many even though the artist may be suggesting something fundamental about life and death.

When artists use faeces, bodily fluids, garbage, cigarette butts or mutated figures in their art they may be offering a very serious response to the way we view life in a sanitised society. Their work may offer a pertinent reflection on the massive waste created by greedy consumer cultures. It may be that the shocking seriousness of environmental destruction being created by humanity today may need to be expressed in equally shocking art work. It is not that human beings are totally removed from waste; we all make it all the time and all of us deal with excrement and bodily fluids on a daily basis. However we become used to dealing with it in a sanitised way; out of sight is out of mind! Only when we are faced with waste in the sanitised environment of a gallery do we actually think about the huge scale of environment waste created by consumer societies. The problem for art teachers is how to show this work to students yet hope that they won't want to create their next art piece out of excrement! One art teacher indicated her concerns about this:

If you offer them this work and start talking about it they may want to use it in their own work that can raise difficulties occasionally, from that point of view it can be difficult.

Highly 'disgusting' art can cause teachers to fear that students will in fact replicate the process. However, some of the art teachers interviewed indicated that this happens rarely and if it does it can be done responsibly. One art teacher described the work of a student who created his own self-portrait using body waste:

This student wanted to do a painting that was related to him without it being illustrative or representational. He found some large trays with various medical instruments in them. Then he started sticking all these trays and medical paraphernalia onto a large board. He then attached plastic bags containing various objects which related to his own person, such as scabby old used bandaids, hair that he had cut off his body, toenails, fingernails, used tissues and other things. It was almost like a set of exhibits at a coroner's inquest, however it was all put up on a wall and called 'art.' It was quite provocative but it was also very liberating for him because he could see how one could make a work which went beyond the expected boundaries of 'school art.' It actually propelled him into another way of thinking which was very liberating for him but also very meaningful. These very good students work very hard on the meaning in their work. It is not just decoration. It goes far beyond that. It becomes a means of communication. It becomes a dialogue. It is meaningful rather than meaningless.

The issue of censorship

For art teachers, media controversy offers a useful starting point for discussion about the role of censorship in art. When the exhibition *Sensations* opened at the Brooklyn Museum of Art, the Mayor of New York publicly denounced it as 'sick' and 'disgusting.' He not only threatened to close the exhibition he also threatened to withhold operating funds to the Museum. However while protestors sang hymns, said rosaries and handed out vomit bags outside the exhibition, others stood in long queues, three hours ahead of opening time, to view the works. The media hype surrounding controversy in art usually raises key issues for critical classroom debate and discussion. It raises the need for students to consider who are the 'gatekeepers' of art in society. It stimulates students to share their views with peers and consider how people of different age groups, cultures, religions or political persuasion may respond to controversial art works. Students need to read the tabloids and weigh up the censorship debate for themselves. Media controversy about art offers excellent fuel for classroom discussion about cutting edge issues when the art world struggles to redefine itself. Censorship is always a cutting edge issue.

Of course, sometimes art gallery directors determine that although a work will be shown to adults it will be censored from young people. The directors of the *Sensations* exhibition issued the following warning when it went on display in the Royal Academy of Arts, London:

There will be works of art on display in the Sensations *exhibition which some people may find distasteful. Parents should exercise their judgment in bringing their children to the exhibition. One gallery will not be open to those under the age of 18.[4]*

This form of public censorship suggests to art teachers that they need to be law abiding when it comes to selecting works for study by students. However, laws of censorship are rarely applied to art works and it is extremely difficult to determine whether a work is, for example, obscene. In Australia censorship laws differ from State to State. In Victoria, for instance, 'it is an offence to exhibit or display an indecent or obscene word, figure or representation in a public place ...'[5] However, in 1992 when the Archbishop of Melbourne applied for an injunction against the National Gallery of Victoria to prevent the opening of the Andres Serrano exhibition, the judge dismissed it suggesting that contemporary standards were largely tolerant of art works, especially those with some artistic merit which are viewed within the context of art galleries. While art teachers are bound to abide by the law of the land and to uphold the charter of the school, most of the time, written laws are too broad and art teachers must work from their own judgment. When in doubt some art teachers simply decide to avoid difficult discussion in the art room by leaving 'distasteful' work out.

Student selection of art works

Most of the fifteen teachers responded with surprise when directly asked if they censor any art works from their teaching programmes. Censorship, as an issue, had not generally been considered. Most art teachers like to think of themselves as liberal and broad-minded and few like to acknowledge that they might engage in some form of censorship. Some teachers initially said they never censored art works but then when probed further suggested that selection of artists for study was up to the students. When art teachers encourage students to self-select the artists and art works they are to study students are encouraged to take responsibility for their own choice. As one art teacher in England explained, a student who developed an interest in body mutilation was allowed to pursue the study but was given guidance in the process:

I have one female student in year 11 who is researching some very disturbing work on body mutilation and artists who suffer pain from hanging themselves from their skin. She has been getting information from the internet and is fascinated yet shocked by it. It is quite horrific to look at her research studies but she is very thoughtful about it and it stemmed from her investigations into Salvador Dalí's work. She has made interesting and intelligent connections between the two. She is now making her own body cast out of latex and stitching it together. It is her intention to suspend it from the ceiling with fish-hooks. We talk about the fact that sometimes art is there to shock. Maybe that is part of its duty to shock. We discuss the need to have some people pushing boundaries.

When students self-select artists for study the teacher still likes to know that the student is treating the topic earnestly and in this case 'thoughtfully' and 'intelligently.' Alarm bells ring when students show signs of replicating the violent, harmful and antisocial processes of the artists they are studying. Most of the teachers interviewed in this study suggested that they like to talk through the 'art of shock' with students. However, not all students will be interested in creating or studying highly contentious art works. Self-selection means that students may study their area of interest without ideas being inflicted on the whole group. Self-selection only fails as a classroom strategy when contentious issues never surface and both students and teachers avoid debate.

Teacher selection of art works

Leaving art works out of the art programme is the most common form of censorship operating in art education. It is not that the art teachers deliberately censor particular artists but they simply choose other artists whom they think will be more inspirational for students. Rather than instigating debate themselves teachers often only raise contentious issues for debate if it first surfaces in the tabloid press or from students' curiosity. As one teacher says:

I haven't deliberately shown any of the students the work of the Chapman brothers. Personally I found their work the most shocking and distasteful in the Sensation exhibition and found it hard to come to terms with. Some other controversial works, such as the Myra Hindley work, were damaged in the Sensation exhibition. Students have some quite strong reactions to works at times especially if they have read things in the tabloid press or their parents have said that the works are shocking and shouldn't be allowed etc. So then you do try to have some kind of discussion and open it up for debate.

Most of the art teachers interviewed suggested that there are particular artists whom they often use in their teaching programmes. These artists are those for which they have personal interest or which they think will lead students further in their own practical art making. These are also artists about whom teachers have collected resources in the form of books, catalogues, articles, videos or CD ROMs. Beyond these materials the internet also provides students with ready access to materials which have not yet appeared in print. Increasingly however, students are accessing images before their teachers. Censoring these materials becomes an increasingly difficult task and teachers are aware that they must be vigilant when it comes to vetting images for student research. Art teachers constantly need to discuss and negotiate the boundaries of art with their students. As Nelson Goodman suggested the issue may not be 'what is art?' but probably 'when is art?'[6]

Dealing with 'irreverence'

Postmodern art is irreverent. Artists often lampoon revered icons of modernist sensibility and challenge fundamental principles of the western canon. Many artists deliberately blur the lines between previously dichotomous artistic notions such as: serious art and kitsch, beauty and horror, male and female, fine art and popular art. Tracey Emin's work *Everyone I Have Ever Slept With 1963–1995, 1995*[7] for example, may seem a blatant and bizarre way to engage in self portraiture. To students, this kind of contemporary work can initially seem trivial, irreverent, even disgusting. It is at this point that art teachers may need to instigate discussion about the usual divide between art and life and the way Emin may be diffusing this divide in her autobiographical works. By deconstructing the Emin work, students can peel away layers of meaning which may be embedded in or evoked by the work. Questioning is vital here as the art teacher leads students to see that postmodern art works may be double-coded; they may initially appear trivial and silly but closer scrutiny reveals that there may be more to them. As one art teacher suggests, students want to know if the artist is serious and this is when interesting debate can occur:

> *What is the work of, for example, Tracey Emin trying to say? Is she making fools of the audience or what is the message that is being communicated? We do talk about these things and students will argue. Some of them really respond positively but they do all have something to say. Some say things like 'Art is going nowhere' or 'It's the skill rather than the idea that matters.' Maybe we would only talk about things that we feel comfortable with ourselves.*

It is at this point also that students can discuss the wider world of art in which the media, dealers, gallery owners and critics etc. interact with artists. Students need only search the web for particular artists and dealers to realise how contemporary artists deliberately manipulate the media to draw attention to their art and contrive responses to it. Many artists construct their own websites and art patrons like Charles Saatchi invest large sums in supporting their artists in the media. In a media saturated world it is no longer possible to know which art works are serious and which are not because many works deliberately fuse these elements together. Generally the teacher has to use his or her own judgment about art and many teachers do censor art works from the curriculum if they sense that they are either a sham, offensive to the students, pornographic or obscene:

> *I realise that I may need to carefully consider some contemporary art which may offend some students but I do not avoid controversy in the art room. I would certainly discuss the British Sensations exhibition, although I am always clear on what I want to achieve from the discussion and I need to be sure the artists are serious about what they are doing. The Piss Christ controversy in Melbourne, for example, raised interesting questions but the selection of that name was done to create effect. I am always clear about this with students and the nature of controversy is worth talking about as well as artistic merits. This school is a conservative school so I use some self-censorship in terms of content when I am talking to a class. In terms of directing*

*students to artists, I have few restrictions, just my personal judgment that they would
benefit from it and can handle it. I use Bill Hensen and his works have some soft-porn
elements. I find kids more shocked by technique than images usually.*

Creating a buffer zone for controversy

One of the central notions of teaching in a postmodern world is the critical
engagement that students will have with considerations of power in art.[8] Within the
art class students can discuss how power serves to privilege some while
simultaneously marginalising others. Deconstruction of art works enables students
to consider how art conveys notions of power, through the representation of gender,
class or culture. Framed within a classroom context in which issues of power are
often discussed, controversial art works can be presented in an inoffensive manner.
When art teachers face issues with students they do not pretend to offer answers
but rather share in the debate which some art works stimulate. One teacher in an
Australian Catholic boys' school described this type of context as a 'buffer zone'; a
supportive context in which students interrogate art works and tease out potential
meanings, purposes and interpretations:

> *In relation to censorship of art works in art education I think the context is important.
> Certainly within the domain of art history and theory we have discussed works such
> as Piss Christ by Andres Serrano and we have looked at it very intelligently I think.
> I have also recently spent a fair bit of time in class discussion Gilbert and George. A
> lot of their recent work is very confronting, concerning bodily fluids and
> homosexuality and other such issues. So I haven't censored that dimension. I do
> however create a certain type of buffer zone when discussing work with students. This
> puts us at a distance so that we can look at such works in a critical way without being
> offended or personally challenged in a negative way.*

The focus on socially critical issues in art classes does concern some art teachers.
The socially critical classroom focuses on interpretation and meanings (semiotics)
more than it focuses on issues of aesthetics (formalism). Some art teachers are
finding that they have to deal with issues that they are not actually trained to teach.
As one teacher suggested:

> *… I don't really see myself as a social engineer in this context. But what we do teach
> when we teach about postmodernism is that social issues are just one of the parameters
> of it.*

This particular teacher recognises that teaching about contemporary art involves
making links with other areas of knowledge. Artists today explore science,
literature, history, robotics, medicine and forensic science with great fascination.
The study of contemporary art can no longer be contained within the narrow
confines of the western or modernist canon and for some this involves a degree of

anxiety as the subject art makes potential curriculum links with subjects such as science, literature, history and social studies. When the subject art moves into the sphere of 'visual culture' it does demand that art teachers rethink the very boundaries of the subject.

When students are ready

Another aspect which concerns art teachers is the 'readiness' of students to deal with contentious issues. One teacher cited Piaget to indicate that students need to be conceptually and emotionally ready to deal with certain issues and that it is inappropriate to introduce students to works which are beyond their current realm of understanding:

There is art that I would not show students. There would have to be. The Chapman brothers work, for example, is censored already in the exhibitions and you have to be 18 to see it. So it is automatically censored, and if it is censored there I cannot allow the students to see it as a teacher. I have to follow the law of the land. We went to the Sensations *exhibition and the Chapman brothers' work was screened off in a separate gallery. And because we took sixth formers quite a few of them could go in and see it. I don't particularly like it. In the* Sensations *exhibition there were little children with penises as noses etc and they are very disturbing. So where do you stand as a teacher introducing students to that? I wouldn't do it. I couldn't lay myself that open. I would be absolutely mad to do it. It would only take one child to say something to a parent and the parent could then check it up etc. It is the sort of thing that is reported on the front page of the Sunday papers.*

…. if you try and take a student through perspective before he is ready for it, it is like showing a dog a card trick. They can follow the actions but it may not actually register. In my B.Ed. work we did a lot of work with Piaget and I am a firm believer that there are kinds of stages. Maybe they are not as ordered and rigid as Piaget defined. But there are points where kids can understand.

Art teachers need to be aware of the need to protect students from potential harm if they consider them to be at risk. Most teachers do carefully select art works for discussion and are careful to avoid offending students or inciting them to violence. One teacher in England mentioned the need to actually keep some art works away from students:

Even with Cindy Sherman's work, I have to be careful about which images I show. I mark the pages to be looked at and I keep that book locked up. I think in the school context it would be wrong to show students some works. What I do depends on the pupil and her interests. I can always say that there is an exhibition on and they can take themselves there.

Studying disorder and dissent

Art teachers who are aware of the complexities involved in teaching students about contemporary art plan art programmes which deliberately deal with issues 'up front.' Some curriculum frameworks recommend introducing students to critical study themes throughout the secondary school. The two teachers from the Australian Catholic School explained their inclusion of 'dissent and disorder' in art as a theme in the syllabus:

> *Last year we looked at dissent and disorder as a theme. Obviously they (the students) not only looked at dissent in modern artists but also in postmodernism. This was a recommended area of study and there is a place in art history for dissent and there are always going to be artists who are pushing the boundaries of accessibility and creating art 'on the edge.' I think it is particularly important for senior students to be aware of the larger picture and if there are art works that question those boundaries then we would look at them. But we would be sensitive and we need to respect the institution we are working in. But I think that the institution would also respect the needs of art.*

Empowering students of the global village

Although this paper has suggested that students may need some protection from potentially offensive or obscene images it may also be the case that some students are extremely aware and concerned about key issues which may seem disgusting in some contexts. There are students who are deeply concerned about global issues related to the environment, economy (debt), migration and the impact of multi-nationalism. A case in point is the Canadian 12-year-old student Craig Kielburger[9] who was profiled in a television documentary for his work as child founder of the *Free the Children* movement, a crusade against child labour. Entitled *It takes a child*, the documentary examined Kielberger's world mission to abolish child slavery. Students, it seems, can have mature and critical ideologies at a young age. Some do see the world's problems seriously and empathise with artists who expose the disgusting side of humanity in their work.

Summary: towards a critical pedagogy

Art teachers know that students will not live in a trouble-free world. They will have to deal with the consequences of consumer culture, mass migration, global warming and the digital revolution. Most art teachers recognise that the art room at school is not a 'safe haven' retreat from reality. The subject 'art' offers a real and potent opportunity to confront reality squarely in the face. Most teachers recognise that students cannot be shielded from the controversial issues which are currently being examined in contemporary art practice. However, art teachers also recognise their responsibility to provide students with a safe 'buffer zone' in which issues of concern can be discussed. It is not that teachers will seek resolution to these issues within this 'buffer zone' but rather that they will develop attitudes of respect and tolerance for diverse opinions and beliefs. Just as art is never actual reality, but rather a semblance of it, the art room is also an environment where the world can be experienced 'virtually.' Through the semblance of 'real life' art students can deal with issues that matter. And the things that matter to the child of the new millennium differ from those that mattered to the child of the previous one. Most of the teachers interviewed in this study do use some form of censorship in their art programmes. They would get themselves into considerable difficulty if they didn't. However, while some art teachers are more 'up front' about dealing with controversy in their art programmes than others, all indicate that they are increasingly moving from a purely 'formalist' approach to a more 'issues-based' or socially critical approach in their art programmes. The issues just won't go away!

Notes and References

1. Television series [2000] *Anatomy of Disgust*. England, Channel 4, 27 August, 10.35 pm.

2. Rosenthal, N. [1997] *Sensation: Young British Artists from the Saatchi Collection*. London: Thames and Hudson/Royal Academy of Arts, p. 11.

3. Sandler, I. [1996] *Art of the Postmodern Era*. NY: Harper Collins, p. 411.

4. Website of Royal Academy of Arts.

5. Website of Arts Law Centre of Australia.

6. Goodman, N. [1976] *Languages of Art: an approach to a theory of symbols*. Indianapolis, Ind.: Hackett.

7. Ibid., note 2, p. 78–79.

8. Aronowitz, S. & Giroux. H. A. [1991] *Postmodern Education: Politics, culture, and social criticism*. Minneapolis: University of Minnesota Press.

9. Television series [2000] *The Big Picture: It Takes a Child*. ABC Television, 23 November, 9:30 pm.

Originally published in the *Journal of Art & Design Education*, volume 21 (1) 2002.

Chapter 4: Post-it Culture: Postmodernism and Art and Design Education

Stuart W MacDonald

Contemporary American and British art education

Currently, there is a trend in the USA, based mostly on a move away from Discipline Based Art Education [DBAE], to invoke postmodernism in curriculum studies in art education. By contrast, there would appear to be relatively little emphasis on postmodernism in the United Kingdom. Whether this is complacency, weariness with continual systemic change, or whether UK models are already postmodern without their being widely known is a moot point. However, this paper uses the American experience as the opportunity to question the relevance of postmodernism as it is applied to art education. This is done neither to negate practice in the USA nor to endorse developments in the UK. It is done as a way of seeking a productive cross comparability between the USA and the UK, to give an enhanced conceptual interpretation of 'international' and 'contemporary' based on the manifest pluralism of present day art and design. Whilst there are underlying reasons for the lack of interest in postmodernism, British art and design education is in as much need of challenge as its American counterpart. Both are struggling with the orthodoxy inherent in the widespread 'nationalisation' of curricula. Rather, this critique is felt necessary in order to enhance the American discourse which, despite the plurality implicit in postmodernism, tends to remain focused in its examples at least on fine art and at best on multiculturalism. The paper seeks to do this comparatively, by taking on board the expanded content available in the best of UK art and design education – design, architecture, media education, and critical and cultural studies.

On the road to attaining some agreement about what postmodernists might offer curriculum developers on both sides of the Atlantic, and before interrogating recent American research, the paper contours the development of postmodernism, drawing in material from design, culture and journalism as well as art. It takes a particular look at the language of postmodernism, at structuralism and semiotics, and queries their generalisability when linked to art and design education. En route, the paper looks at the most recent work of one of the important referents of American postmodern art educationists, Arthur Danto. Thus privileged, several strategies are posited for future development of which postmodernism is but one. In true postmodernist fashion, the paper revisits and reanimates some earlier post-war ideas for consideration such as creativity, visual literacy and Basic Design, so strengthening the need for historical studies in art and design education.

Postmodernism or postmodernisms?

Few 'isms' have provoked as much perplexity and suspicion as postmodernism. In his set of essays Adair[1] asks, if one is capable of recognising *Batman* as a postmodern film and Richard Rogers' Lloyds building as postmodern architecture, how can such dissimilar things have anything in common? Furthermore, when postmodernism is applied to art and design education, as is the recent case in the USA by Efland, Freedman and Stuhr, what is one to make of it?[2] The sole consensus it would appear is that modernism has in Adair's words 'spluttered out',[3] 'failed' as Gablick[4] would have it or, according to Harvey, 'destroyed' itself.[5] In other words, the grand narratives or meta-narratives that shaped the progressive thrust of modernism through most of this century have lost credibility. Architecture especially, is regarded as representing that loss of faith; post-war housing schemes which failed to achieve their modernist inspired dreams of social harmony being one commonly cited instance. Charles Jencks, the architectural critic and protagonist of postmodernism, has recently reasserted its worldliness, variety and pluralism.[6] Moreover, Jencks is credited by many commentators with the term 'double-coding,' with incorporating the past and the present, with mixing different styles – at its most recognisable in postmodern buildings. Double-coding permits the idea of postmodern politics, of postmodern food, even postmodern horticulture, and is a potentially important idea in art and design education.

British cultural studies

Postmodernism has a parallel with post-industrialisation, with what Eco has called 'the end of an age of innocence',[7] and what Foucault has termed the 'post-modern condition'.[8] In that sense, in the UK, there has been an evident interest in urban regeneration and social renewal. However, rather than travel well worn sources – French structuralists like Foucault, Derrida, Barthes – this paper utilises an indirect source, the 'aura' of postmodernism as seen through cultural commentary and critical studies. Adair, for example, has drawn another parallel, with 'creative stocktaking,' with archival interest in the past, and has contrasted these more serious concerns with the superficiality of the 'post-it,' cut and paste menu of much of the deconstruction that travels under the portmanteau term of postmodernism.[9] Furthermore, Adair has defined culture as 'applied art,' meaning that the work of art becomes a work of culture only when it been 'externalised, extrapolated from, thought about, talked about, read about, communicated and shared.' Adair further argues that the arts exist principally to fuel the culture industry, to furnish the gregariousness of the cultural discourse with a constantly replenished and potentially inexhaustible supply of referents. Far from being pessimistic, his perception is of a growing democratisation. Cultural literacy in Adair's terms is about familiarity with art derived almost exclusively, not from the work itself – be it theatre, painting or opera – but from the aura given off by the thousands of reviews about it. Discussion of culture in this context is useful for, not only does it negate the idea that art is dead: far from it – more and more art is being produced – but indicates also that specialised venues such as theatres, galleries, auditoria become less important than free connectivity; increasingly, art will come to us.

The paradigm shift is from mass production to mass consumption, with culture evermore becoming the site of contention, for political, social and other debates mediated through the language and images of the arts – a locus for values and judgment no less. This is most pronounced and best observed where the edges between art forms blur, for example, in performance and installation but also, it is suggested, where culture is used as a vehicle for social and economic renewal. Hewison, the British cultural historian has, however, pointed up the inherent dangers in the commodification of culture, of what he has termed 'public culture,' serving the interests of the arts hegemony in the form of the Arts Council, for example.[10] Nonetheless, it is interesting to note that in Glasgow – Britain's foremost example of post-industrial reclamation, a city which is successfully reinventing itself through culture – ephemeral art forms are pre-eminent, many of them in open opposition to 'public culture.' In that postmodern case study the official and unofficial co-exist; it is double-coded. What education has to learn is that, in Macluhan's terms, not only is the message suspect but the medium could be as well, postmodern discourse included, especially when the concept of literacy is involved.

Reading semiotics

The concept of 'reading,' meaning in the semiotician's terms – interpretation, decoding and deciphering – has been crucial to the postmodern debate. As a method of reading, deconstruction moved from literary texts to film, to architecture and then the visual arts. Despite the democratising utility in shifting the emphasis from 'writer' to 'reader,' and despite its popularity with postmodern art educators,[11] the literary metaphor may encounter problems when extended to the visual arts and design. It cannot be assumed that all writings, 'écriture,' are the same. Design theory and history is an especial case. Being a relatively young discipline there is an assumption behind the world's reduction into 'text' that there is a developed language for talking about design objects such as chairs. Arguably, there is not in the same way that there is a critical discourse for architecture or fine art.[12] Whilst it is not debated that Cubist pictures may be read in the sense that they can be recognised as such, this is more by habituation. 'Ecriture' has not made the meaning of Cubist pictures any more transparent.

Nevertheless, reading can also be conceptualised as 'programming,' what Adair refers to as the casual disruption or dislocation of a work to suit one's own rhythms. Video-recording and playback or the use of a music CD are but two examples; 'surfing the net' is an even more extreme case. These freedoms permit greater authorship, what Willis has referred to in the case of young people's participation as 'creative consumption,' as 'grounded aesthetics'.[13] There is insufficient space here to do justice to the richness and potential of this area. What is remarkable about it compared to the debate about postmodernism and the curriculum is the banality of the models that are erected. The debate may be not so much about the repudiation of modernism and the championship of cultural diversity, but more to do with the legitimisation of the richness of the common culture of young people and the recognition of its role in the curriculum.

The fact is that, more and more, culture will be something that happens in our own space, may be less and less to do with artists and their intentions and, increasingly, may involve reproductions and interventions at many stages removed from the original work. This is happening anyway, for despite the growth in critical studies and gallery education, research indicates that young people do not frequent art galleries.[14] It may be, however, that their creativity is being made manifest in other ways. Possibly, art galleries will become like reference libraries, where occasionally people go to see the patina of a rare original. Does this mean that art – and perhaps art and design education is dead?

Arthur Danto – after the end of art

Of all the philosophers referred to by art and design commentators on postmodernism, Danto is arguably one of the most serviceable. Much of this stems from his essay *The End of Art*[15] in which, famously, he used the example of Warhol's *Brillo Box* to say that as anything could be a work of art you had to turn from sense experience to thought, in other words, to philosophy. According to Danto, for the Brillo Box to raise the question 'why am I a work of art?' was to signify the end of modernism because it was too material, too aesthetic, too concerned with pure painting, too un-contextualised to address such a question. But at the same time it signaled the possibility of a serious philosophy of art and thus, by association, art education.

Therefore, the grand historical narrative of modernism was over, to be supplanted with a range of minor narratives. In terms of art and design education, Efland *et al.* have not only provided a comparison of modernism and postmodernism but also assigned a role for 'little narratives as a model for curricula'.[16] Nevertheless, Danto's original paradigm shift (occasioned by the end of art) – the move from purely aesthetic considerations coupled with the need to think about art – has ramifications for contemporary curriculum studies in art and design education, especially in giving critical studies the role seen by some as central.[17]

Danto has updated what he has described as a 'vaguely formulated idea of the end of art,' stating not that there will be no more art but that such art as there might be will be 'post-historical'.[18] This is his preferred term – and this is profoundly important for any critique of a postmodernist approach to art and design because postmodernism closely designates a style. One can pick out postmodern objects: a Gehry building, a Schnabel painting, an Arad chair. Further, to talk of postmodernisms is, in Danto's terms, to lose this recognitional ability and, thus, the possibility of a narrative direction. As Danto would describe it, postmodernism is one narrative amongst many post-historical narratives. If we accept that art can be anything and is highly pluralistic, the question is not 'what does a postmodern art education look like?', but 'what might a post-historical art education resemble?' Danto's belief that, after the end of art, the pluralism and tolerance of the contemporary art world ought to be a harbinger of political things to come, has an important message for art education.

Postmodern art education

Although it may not be desirable, even if such a thing were possible, to say that art education had attained narrative closure like modernism, art educationists have attempted to link the orthogonal of twentieth century art education with modernism, albeit from a North American perspective. Much of the focus of this work has been on appropriating models from postmodern thought in order to inform curriculum studies or to teach about postmodernism itself. For example, teaching about postmodernism has identified montage and image appropriation as a way of reflecting the pluralism and diversity of postmodern life.[19] And, in terms of curriculum, multiculturalism, and the range of approaches possible under that heading, have emerged as a result of modernism being seen as exclusive and postmodernism culturally inclusive.[20] The same analysis has also erected 'little narratives' and other postmodernisms such as deconstruction and 'double-coding' as relevant curriculum issues.[21] These are legitimate contributions, and deserve wider recognition as they are capable of privileging policy development in art and design education, internationally. The issue is, of course, that they represent but one narrative and it may be that several other narratives are possible.

This can be seen in the models that Efland *et al.* offer by way of introducing postmodern concepts into the classroom.[22] These range in contexts from the multicultural (study of Native American Pow Pow) to popular culture (study of postcards). There is no space here to do an in-depth critique of these case-studies, but their complexity and range reinforce Danto's view that postmodernism is inappropriately wide and that multiculturalism, for example, is a post-historical narrative in its own right. Chalmers' recent research underpins this.[23] His conclusion that we need to ask questions of 'ourselves, our students, the curriculum and the environments in which we teach' and of the need to celebrate diversity in art and in life parallels Danto, namely, that after the end of art one of art's main functions is addressing its audiences and their life-streams. In a critique of different forms of art education, Mason supports this view but goes further, arguing for a wider range of role models than the 'artist, aesthetician, art critic and historian'.[24] Mason's thesis concerns the exclusion of artisan and craftspeople –

roles associated with folk art and with ethnic cultures – and is predicated on an anthropological approach to curriculum. To these one could also add the exclusion of the culture of young people themselves. Clearly, such a breadth of views and issues cannot simply be subsumed under the mantle of postmodernism.

The post-medium age

Adding to the emerging complexity of postmodernism, Hal Foster has raised the interesting notion of a 'post-medium' age.[25] Foster refers to a delimiting post-war modernism which was particularly medium, or discipline/medium, specific. This he contrasts with the pluralism of the current situation which is more debate, discourse or even context specific. As an idea it does have some utility to art and design education in schools, especially when applied to the subject's preoccupation with the practical domain. Nevertheless, given the lack of apparent interest in postmodernism, certainly amongst practitioners, it is unlikely that the notion of a 'post-medium' art and design education could attain much currency, although it does enhance the argument for an expanded range of narratives.

Other narratives

Nonetheless, there is little room for complacency in the various UK national curricula – each suffers from examination systems which encourage orthodoxy. There are, however, innovative examples which, when correlated with the recent work of Efland *et al.*, might extend the range of available case-studies. One example is 'issue-based' art and design education, which in Foster's terms would be discourse specific. In that context, Binch and Clive have produced a series of case-studies demonstrating the unexpected outcomes that can result in encounters between artists, young people and the external environment.[26] Such work highlights the cogency of collaboration and co-operation. Another example is design education. The reputation of Britain's art schools in producing some of the world's best fashion, product, graphic and textile designers is legendary. Design education is rooted in the curriculum of schools throughout the UK and its process-based approach involving student evaluation at crucial stages is an example of democratisation and negotiated learning. Media studies is yet another instance. Media studies and media-based approaches have a long history in the UK, especially in Scotland.[27] Such studies have opened up opportunities for breaking down stereotypes and examining different forms of representation. But probably the most significant examples can be found at the interface between art and design education and the public realm, where both are involved in the process of community regeneration through culture (context specific). Glasgow's civic rehabilitation is again a case in point. Slogans such as 'art for regeneration's sake' and 'Changing Glasgow by Design' whilst demonstrating, literally, the invention of new mini-narratives, signal important programmatic shifts. One concerns the inter-relationship of art, architecture and design. As Kirkpatrick, a designer heavily involved in Glasgow's renaissance, has remarked:

I believe that 'architects' and fine artists are also 'designers' as we share the same creative process before we are named after a specific specialist skill such as 'sculptor', 'architect' or 'graphic designer.' I firmly believe that artists, architects and designers would find it easier to explain their usefulness to other members of society, if only they would recognise the common ground they share rather than pigeon holing themselves according to their preferred specialism.[28]

Urban programmes that put creativity to the fore and which involve interactions between schools and art, design and architecture professionals, add to that utility.

The selected examples above are all little narratives – they are all post-historical (and post-medium). This is not to say that postmodernism has been internalised by British art educators. Rather, the examples demonstrate that there is some pluralism at work within the system. In a postmodern or post-historical sense if they were recognised as little narratives, that there was no meta-narrative such as child-centred expression, and also no competition between subjects, a more enlightened humanistic curriculum design might result.

What is evident is the need for more international research in contemporary art education that goes beyond superficial characteristics and recognises why there are national differences as well as indicating instances of potential synergy. If, as Danto suggests, there is a need for a philosophy which can interrogate the question, 'what is art?' then consideration of Discipline Based Art Education (DBAE) and critical studies becomes crucial.

Critical studies and DBAE: the need for a philosophical narrative

Given the approximation of British critical studies and American DBAE, and possible disenchantment with the latter occasioning a move to embrace postmodernism, it is impossible to avoid discussing the differences between the two. As Swift has remarked, although DBAE and critical studies derived from the same theoretical base, critical studies has progressed differently; it has not rigidly followed the discipline-based argument. Instead, it has attempted to interweave the various elements in an 'interactive and overall learning experience.'[29] The simplistic arguments between making and understanding, and about weighting which 'plagues' DBAE have been eschewed. Swift has argued that critical studies has much greater potential than DBAE because it privileges practical work and that artists' residencies linked to the development of critical studies have provided a substantial platform for progress.

There is also evidence in the UK of a precursor to critical studies being used in what might be described as a postmodern strategy. In Scotland, in the Fifties, several policy documents advocated for the use of art appreciation as a means of ameliorating the worst effects of child self-expression.[30] Scotland is an interesting case-study in another respect. Apart from its people always having been culturally diverse Scots, Gaels, Norse, Picts, Celts – its education system has avoided the extremes of ideology evident in the more discipline-centred debates within the English system, for example, about Basic Design or cross arts. In Scotland the focus has therefore been settled on the needs of the learner and the milieu in which he or she learns. Art and design education has profited from such a 'post-synthetic' condition. This too is a post-historical narrative, transcending as it does subject hierarchies.

The lesson is that we can all learn from each other and achieve what Swift calls a 'richer cultural consciousness' – in curriculum terms a permanent, permeating critical programme. The narrative for that programme needs to be as pluralistic as the contemporary art and design which constitutes its context. It should draw on and make manifest the approaches inherent in other mini-narratives: philosophical enquiry; multiculturalism; cultural studies; media studies; feminism, as well as postmodernism. The beauty of this is that the examples already exist – they can be extrapolated from within existing resources.

One site for this programme might be the last remaining educational meta-narrative: standards and the myth of their perceived efficacy across time and place. If art and design is not postmodern any more than it was modernistic, it might be said to be in a post-narrative phase. Despite the delegation that has occurred in the last decade or so – in general terms, Local Management of Schools (LMS) and the school development planning movement or in subject terms, the variety of forms of making education has never been more centralised and bureaucratic. It could be argued postmodernistically that this is 'double-coding,' or one could continue to argue that the demise of centralised approaches are overdue and are inconsistent with the pluralism of contemporary life. At least in the case of art and design there are pragmatic ways already available to take this critical philosophy forward. Chalmers' questions embedded within an approach to cultural pluralism[31] and Mason's discussion of a 'whole school approach' to multiculturalism,[32] are but two examples targeted on the subject and school, respectively.

The regeneration of critical studies: cultural literacy

Various efforts have been made to regenerate critical studies including most recently its strategic re-titling as 'critical literacy',[33] or restructuring as 'Integrated Studies.'[34] Both reveal a semantic attempt to find a contemporary resonance. Neither, however, addresses the tendentious range of demands indicated earlier. The postmodernism, 'multiple readings' – ways of questioning different sources that give rise to several different answers – are not fully accommodated by these neologisms. Adair's identification of 'cultural literacy' and his notion of culture as 'applied art' may possess greater utility. It may also, in the spirit of recuperation evident in at least one reading of postmodernism,[35] be capable of absorbing and sustaining some earlier ideas. Visual literacy, which grew out of the didacticism of Fifties Basic Design, is a clear front-runner. Clive has given an account of the development of Visual Literacy in Britain, correlating it with American and Australian studies, coupled with a survey of approaches to the subject.[36] Her conclusion is that a range of languages or literacies are at work and that it means encouraging diversity and unique local initiatives; all quite consistent with postmodern rehabilitation.

Similarly, Basic Design, which developed from William Johnstone's pre-war contacts with the Bauhaus and post-war pioneering at the Camberwell and Central Schools of Art, and which had the possibility of counteracting the prevalence of untutored child expression, still holds out possibilities. Although it became academicised, its over-formality incapable of synthesising individual creativity, Thistlewood has logged the creative dimension of this movement, particularly in relation to Hudson, Pasmore and Hamilton's resolution of opposites.[37] This was the 'New Creativity' which combined 'grammar' with three-dimensional construction, popular culture and performance art, and could be the seed of an important fresh narrative. Creativity itself, which in the past, according to Taylor and Andrews[38] has been mishandled due to its being seen as the generic 'core' in rationalising the arts in schools, has also been given a new focus. This has come about because of the interest in cultural renewal as an engine of economic regeneration. It has been applied to cities[39] in which context the idea of 'synthetic creativity' has been coined with reference to a 'climate of creativity' meaning a soft set of skills, and sets a postmodern challenge that opposites can be parts of the same whole. It is another element in the reprogramming of critical studies to become more culturally applicable and diverse.

Conclusion

Postmodernism, in its most definitive state is an authentic architectural style and at its least defined a broadly described 'condition,' has now been appropriated by contemporary art curriculum commentators. This has been done to seek a new direction away from the over concentration on DBAE in the same way that postmodernism was used to mitigate the restrictions of modernism. Postmodernism is attractive, certainly as an antidote to the universal prescription of many national curricula. However, in one sense, the 'condition' has been utilised to become a 'perspective'[40] but the breadth of the latter is such that only multiculturalism – in itself a very broad approach – can be offered as a staple component of that view. And, at least one commentator[41] has indicated that an emphasis on multiculturalism and DBAE are quite compatible – parts of the same whole? Postmodernism is not a single narrative but one amongst many post-historical narratives. Critical studies provides the best platform for contextualising experiences in the art room, and by offering the idea of several 'literacies,' could promote a wider understanding of a range of cultures. Postmodernism can aid the re-rationalisation of critical studies by endowing novel concepts and approaches, and cultural literacy may offer a wider brief. Furthermore, this discussion of postmodernism has introduced the idea of a range of narratives and the importance of a variety of critiques, including philosophical enquiry. It has also served as an indicator, using the postmodern example of cultural diversity, that national systems of art and design education, despite superficial similarities, are different and that they represent different narratives. It also indicates how post-historical art and design education is dependent on a widening of art educational historiography and needs to reanimate some earlier debates.

'Creative stocktaking' has shown that the expropriation of postmodernism by some art educationists may be of less value than highlighting the need for consensus about a new form of critical studies that fully integrates multiculturalism along with recuperative debates about creativity and visual literacy. Whether this is organised under 'cultural literacy' or any other form, the recognition that there are a range of narratives is the key. What are needed are post-narrative guidelines for an enlarged art and design education for the new millennium. The programme ought to be the pluralism and internationalism of contemporary art, design and architecture itself.

Notes and References

1. Adair, G. [1992] *The Post-Modernist Always Rings Twice*. Cambridge University Press.

2. Efland, A., Freedman, K. and Stuhr, p. [1996] *Postmodern Art Education: an approach to curriculum*. Virginia USA: National Art Education Association.

3. Adair, op. cit.

4. Gablick, S. [1984] *Has Modernism Failed?* New York: Thames and Hudson.

5. Harvey, D. [1989] *The Condition of Postmodernity, an enquiry into the origins of social change*. Oxford: Basil Blackwell.

6. Jencks, C. [1996] *What is Post-modernism?* London: Academy Editions.

7. Eco, U. [1984] *Reflections on the Name of the Rose*. Harcourt Brace.

8. Foucault, M. [1970] *The Order of Things: an archeology of the human sciences*. New York: Random House.

9. Adair, op. cit.

10. Hewison, R. [1995] *Culture and Consensus England, Art and Politics since 1940*. London: Methuen.

11. Efland et al., op. cit., p. 106.

12. Sudjic, D. [1996] keynote presentation, Design Matters Seminar, Glasgow School of Art.

13. Willis, P. [1990] *Moving Culture*. London: Calouste Gulbenkian Foundation.

14. Harland, J., Kinder, K., and Hartley, K. [1996] *Arts in their View – a study of youth participation in the arts*. London: NFER.

15. Danto, A. 'The End of Art' in Lang, B. (ed.) [1984] *The Death of Art*, New York: Haven Publishers.

16. Efland et al., op. cit.

17. Hughes, A. 'Creating Cross-curricular Connections' in Prentice, R. (ed.) [1995] *Teaching Art and Design*. London: Cassell.

18. Danto, A. [1997] *After the End of Art*. Princeton University Press.

19. Haynes, D. J. [1995] *Teaching Postmodernism*. Art Education, September, vol 48, no 20.

20. Efland et al., op. cit.

21. Ibid. Efland et al. refer to Jencks' use of the term 'double coding' to indicate how a building can incorporate both historical and contemporary styles.

22. Efland et al., op. cit., pp. 118–37.

23. Chalmers, G. F. [1996] *Celebrating Pluralism*. Getty Centre for Education in the Arts.

24. Mason, R. [1995] *Art Education and Multiculturalism*. Corsham, NSEAD.

25. Interview with Hal Foster, Variant. Glasgow, summer 1997.

26. Binch, N. and Clive, S. [1994] *Close Collaborations*. Arts Council of Great Britain.

27. MacDonald, S. [1997] *Remembering the Future: Art and Design and Media Education in Scotland*, Journal of Art & Design Education, vol 16, no 1.

28. Kirkpatrick, J. [1997] *Design as a Tool for Cultural Change: Glasgow's Experience*, Journal of Art & Design Education, vol 16, no 1.

29. Swift, J. 'Critical Studies: A Trojan Horse' in Dawtrey E. et al. (eds.) [1996] *Critical Studies and Modern Art*. Yale University Press.

30. See for example: SED [1956] *The Teaching of Art in Secondary Schools*. Edinburgh, HMSO.

31. Chalmers, op. cit.

32. Mason, R. *Beyond Tokenism: Towards Criteria for Evaluating the Quality of Multicultural Art Curricula, Art Education and Multiculturalism*, op. cit.

33. Buchanan, M. 'Making Art and Critical Literacy: a Reciprocal Relationship' in Prentice, R. (ed.) [1995] *Teaching Art and Design*, London: Cassell.

34. SOEID [1996] *Higher Still – Art and Design*. Edinburgh, HMSO.

35. Fuller, P. 'Aesthetics After Modernism' in Abbs, P. (ed.) [1989] *The Symbolic Order*. London: Falmer.

36. Clive, S. 'Thoughts on Visual Literacy' in Binch, N. and Clive, S. [1994] *Close Collaborations*.

37. Thistlewood, D. 'A Continuing Process: The New Creativity in British Art Education 1955–65' in Thistlewood, D. (ed.) [1992] *Histories of Art and Design Education*. Harlow, Longman/NSEAD.

38. Taylor, R. and Andrews, G. [1993] *The Arts in the Primary School*. London: Falmer.

39. Biancini, F. and Landry, C. [1995] *The Creative City*. London: DEMOS.

40. Efland et al., op. cit.

41. Chalmers, op. cit.

Originally published in the *Journal of Art & Design Education*, volume 17 (3) 1998.

Chapter 5: The Trouble with Postmodernism

Stuart W MacDonald

Introduction

This paper is less concerned with recherché formulations of postmodern philosophy than with culture or milieu. In that sense, it seeks to propel the debate about postmodernism and art and design education that I introduced in JADE 17.3.[1] That paper drew on Danto's [1984] critique of modernism's end, his observation that Warhol's *Brillo Box* work heralded the end of art because modernism was too aesthetic, too bothered with personal expression, too medium specific to deal with it, so, necessitating a move from sensory experience to thought process, to a new philosophy of art.[2] Danto described this phase as 'post-historical' and called for a renewed utilisation of the idea of the contemporary in art seeing Postmodernism – or 'Post-modernisms' – as lacking optimism or narrative direction, both of which, arguably, are inexorable parts of the educational process. The former paper was also critical of emerging American postmodern curricula being too 'folksy' in content or over-concentrated on multiculturalism.[3] Equally, in the UK, Issues-based Art Education, seemed to stem from an ideological desire to counter examination driven orthodoxies rather than from a priori philosophies appropriate for their time. For instance, Eagleton has remarked that postmodernism can be as censorious and exclusive as the orthodoxies it opposes.[4] Lastly, there was the pervading criticism that the debate, whether centred in the USA or the United Kingdom, is too focused on fine art to the exclusion of design, architecture or media studies. Indeed, Foster has added to our sense of an enhanced definition of postmodernism through his notion of a post-medium age,[5] indicating that modernist discourse was very discipline specific, no longer capable of addressing the range of contemporary art.

Two substantive issues emerged, it seemed, from observation of the debate about what a postmodern curriculum might be. One was the lack of a coherent philosophy, possibly caused by the promiscuity of the concept. The other was an over-emphasis on the content of any postmodern curriculum and perceived external constraints on art education as opposed to the learning methodologies that might enliven it. This paper utilises Danto's and Foster's philosophies. In addition, it raises a number of new or regenerated skills drawn from a reconceptualisation of creativity as well as anthropology and archaeology. All of these permeate and characterise what is current in art, architecture and design, giving rise to an integrated view of contemporary practice. Moreover, the paper suggests instead of a grand narrative a grand dialogue to advance models and methods that might reasonably attract the interest of those ultimately responsible for implementing a curriculum that is relevant for the new millennium, teachers of the visual arts. The theme is the environment but in the context of everyday culture.

The paper therefore starts with an idea – the Museum of the Ordinary – as a way of encapsulating the debate and rooting it in contemporary life. Against that backdrop some new skills are offered in relation to the needs of life-long learners. Several models are then illustrated as a way of not only bridging the sectoral divide and inter-relating all the visual arts – art, design and architecture but integrating art and life. This is done by outlining examples in which theory is seen as valuable as practice; crucially, practice that transcends disciplinary boundaries. It also looks at the commodification of culture as a concern of critics, artists and educators.

The Museum of the Ordinary

Throughout the twentieth century numerous commentators have called for greater attention to be paid to the environment. Charles Rennie Mackintosh's mentor, Fra Newbery, was vocal about such things well before the Great War. Post 1945 reports on art education called for a greater interaction with the external world, but with little success.[6] As we near the millennium, at one level, Willis has stated that only by releasing the energies and talents of young people will the public realm and our post-industrial inner cities be revitalised.[7] At another, Swift has appealed for thorough-going curriculum change criticising present-day art education that eschews the environment and public forms of art in favour of safer modes.[8] The aspiration permeating all of these has been the desire to relate art to life, but the isolation of schools from the communities they inhabit persists. In many instances this has been exacerbated by the perceived 'difference' or mystique surrounding the art world, including museums and galleries, and the hegemony of fine art practice in schools. All of these are institutionalised practices which apparently have a decreasing relevance to the lives of young people.[9]

An interesting model has been proposed by graphic artists Rock and Sellars – the Museum of the Ordinary – based on the urban grid of Manhattan.[10] Its spaces are above and below street level. Its collection consists of all the designed objects within the perimeter of the museum and encompasses facades, rooftops, posters, T-shirts, graffiti, street theatre. In fact it is so large that the 'curators' are responsible for dividing it into units that follow the urban grain. Costs are non-existent, cataloguing the space is continuous and circulation routes through it flexible and numerous. 'Exhibitions' can reflect the curators' tastes – design, public art, architecture, vandalism, traffic flow, consumerism, food, street theatre, multi-media, fashion, biology. Whilst the example of Manhattan is rich and ever-changing in content, the lesson is nevertheless clear – any area is capable of becoming the Museum of the Ordinary. The concept holds out a range of democratising ideas. Everyone can be a curator, collector, connoisseur, interventionist. And, as a depository of objects for study it is infinite. Moreover, as a context for learning, the knowledge it is capable of creating is huge.

The wonderful thing about the Museum of the Ordinary is that it is a theory without a practice, an empty frame. It answers a postmodern desire for plurality but gives a focus without being prescriptive. In art educational terms it is more than a resume of Art and the Built Environment (ABE) or a 'local area study.'[11] If the traditional museum is about the control of space and meaning, the Museum of the Ordinary is about the release of that control. The former is about order, the latter celebrates diversity. The museum extracts art or design as an autonomous object, the Museum of the Ordinary sees art and design as a practice without exteriority. 'As it is ultimately nothing, it allows us to fill it with everything.'[12]

Anthropology and archaeology

The Museum of the Ordinary is an engaging and empowering idea because of its democratisation of content. The history of art education in the twentieth century, however, is littered with a succession of ideas each appearing to offer more than the previous one. Environmentally based schemes are no exception. Most recently, Critical Studies, perceived by many to offer a bridge between theory and practice, between school art and the world of art, between classroom and the environment, is now seen as a problem.[13] But unlike ABE, it has been absorbed into and rendered orthodox by the system.

But whilst art education in schools has become more and more introverted, art in HE has changed radically because of its apparently closer relationship with professional practice, as discussed by Hughes,[14] for example. That practice has become less aesthetically and individualistically dominated and is more culturally based. Directly or indirectly, it draws on disciplines like cultural anthropology which is closely linked to archaeology, and which fuses theory and method, looks at the social nature of the production of artefacts and has close links with both the new art and design history. It is a common denominator, especially video anthropology, in much contemporary art, design and architecture.

Douglas Gordon's site-specific work located in Glasgow's Merchant City, *Empire* [Figure 1], is a case in point. At first glance it is evocative of the many Art Deco cinema or dance hall signs in the city, some of which survive; indeed it is in sympathy with the neon pub signs in the same street. But it is attached to a blank wall, not any identifiable building. Because of the narrowness of the street, which is just off one the city's busiest shopping thoroughfares, it is impossible – even if one wished – to look at the work in isolation. Next, one is aware that the word 'Empire' is reversed (on either side). The perception grows that this is a work of art because it cannot be anything else. The colonialist connection between Empire and the Merchant City is made whilst recognising at the same time that The

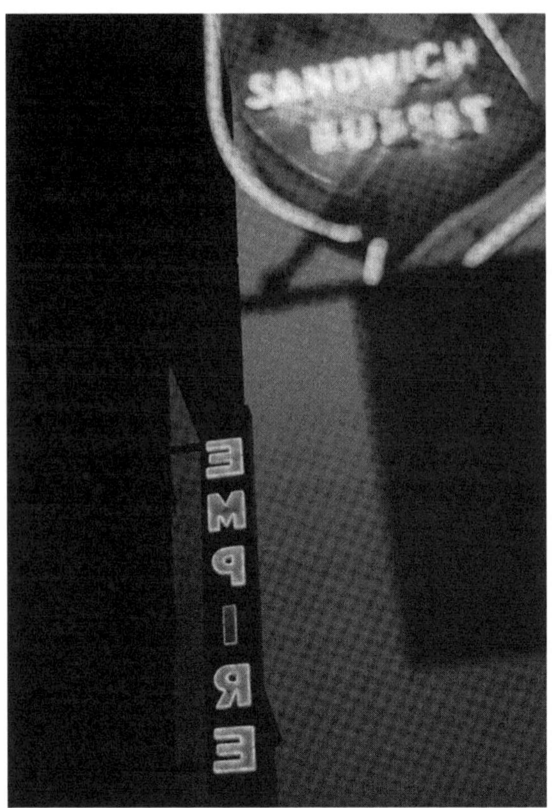

Douglas Gordon 'Empire' site specific work, Glasgow
(picture by Lucy Byatt, 1999, Visual Art Projects)

Merchant City is a property marketing construct – this was the city's warehouse district. Nonetheless, the allusion and the city's imperialist role resonates. There is also the association between Empire and empirical which is the way in which the sign is being studied. Empire is capable of a multiple reading because it exists as image and reality. Then, there is the feeling of loss whether loss of Empire, the loss of the Second City's commercial heyday, or the desolation of the urban fabric, including the incompletion of the Merchant City. But there is the notion of reversal.

As some anthropologists put it, culture is a toolkit of techniques and procedures for managing and understanding the world. As Bruner says, what is important is the procedure of enquiry, of mind using, which is central to cultural democracy.[15] It is clear that to produce and interpret a work such as *Empire* requires a cultural literacy that is a million miles away from school art. Nonetheless, there are examples in the school sector. Kim Boyle is one artist whose practice is dedicated to environmental work and to the study of the interactions that are necessarily involved in large-scale environmental art and design projects. Boyle's aspiration was to involve both primary and secondary pupils in a mapping and photographic study of their area (Drumchapel, the housing scheme in which she herself grew up) – the Museum of the Ordinary perhaps. And, she wanted the work to culminate in a full-size billboard that would be placed in Drumchapel and become part of the environment. The process revealed the inhibiting nature of much school-based art and design because in this context fieldwork, site visits, large-scale mapping, teamwork, crit-sessions, photography, computer work – and, importantly, cross-phase and cross-sector working – were innovations. The project involved working with a graphic designer as well as the artist, and a local FE college. In Danto's terms the children made 'an art of their own.' The billboard which was sited in the city centre as well as Drumchapel was in its way as worthy of study as Gordon's *Empire*. Neither Gordon nor Boyle allow themselves to be represented by the conventional narratives of art or art education. In both there is an affinity with the concept of the Museum of the Ordinary and the anthropology needed to animate that context; a new mini-narrative in other words.

Little miracles and little narratives: Glasgow School of Art's environmental art course

The phenomenon of a dynamic centre upon which young artists such as Douglas Gordon and many others like Boyle with a commitment to developing art with the community, converge or choose to stay has repeatedly been referred to by curator Hans Olrich Obrist as the 'Glasgow miracle.'[16] A lot of these young artists are graduates of the Environmental Art course set up by Harding at the Glasgow School of Art (GSA). Harding has been instrumental in creating a discourse about 'public art education' which he refers to as 'public art, contentious term and contested practice.'[17] The most important aspect of this course is that it is as much philosophical as practical, illuminated by its appropriation of the maxim of the Artists' Placement Group 'the context is half the work.' As Ainsley, who taught on the course for five years, has remarked:

Students who were still only in their teens or early twenties, drew attention to the spaces and situations in their city on a number of levels; moral, social, economic, political or spiritual, giving neither answers nor preaching, but rather, grappling with art and ideas about its place in society.[18]

The course demands amongst other things that students locate a space or site, research the context as well as undertake evaluation and documentation, answering the challenge to make work that reinterprets and broadens attitudes, remaining at the same time sensitive to the users of the site.

As well as producing graduates like Gordon, the example of the course and the debates it has engendered are very germane to secondary art education, especially the philosophical line on context. Of greater importance, however, is the anticipation of Foster's idea of the 'post-medium' and the prescient investigative and interpretive methodologies that have been developed. They go a long way to answer demands for anthropological approaches which avoid the grand narrative of twentieth century art education – the ideology of individualism and an over-emphasis on the aesthetic. Not least, they combine theory and practice. The work of Christine Borland, another graduate of GSA, is again a case in point. Borland's work has been described as a form of 'social archaeology.'[19] It emphasises 'interpretation over excavation' and is absorbed with context, so shifting the site of the debate from artist to audience and from definitions of art to definitions of society.

Nor is the idea confined to fine art. Kirkpatrick, a Glasgow designer, curator and critic, believes that we can't change culture, only interpret it in new ways:

> *… it is important that cities, especially post-industrial cities, such as Glasgow, use design as a tool for cultural change, providing an analytical framework through which to understand the archaeology of the past and describe what the archaeology of the future might be.*[20]

However, it is one thing to point to models or methods in terms of the post-historical or post-medium, it is quite another to influence teachers or policy-makers. This is not to say, for example, that GSA's efforts to bridge the sectoral gulf, including an extensive, long-running student artist-in-schools scheme and wide-ranging InSET activities, have had no effect. They have. The problem is much more deeply rooted. It needs an attitudinal change on the part of both artists and art educators.

Cultural rights

Part of the present difficulty is the limited definition of art and the need to move beyond the aristocratically established forms of the nineteenth century to embrace the urban cultures of the twentieth. As Mulgan has argued:

> *Concentrating on pre-twentieth century forms inevitably means concentrating on cultural products that were originally created for a wealthy, minority audience.*[21]

Schools have perpetuated that state of affairs, hence the still life as the staple diet of art courses in schools. The other part of the problem is the need to break out of the ghetto made by contemporary artists and their critics. The walls of this ghetto according to Hewison, are constructed 'from an obscure technical language,' and he has demanded that contemporary artists and critics:

> *… abandon their own grand, masterly narratives, and engage in the difficulties, limitations, contingencies, specificities, anecdotes, and contradictions of raw material experience. A few jokes would help to open up the absurdity of the way things are.*[22]

As Horne sees it for many people art is something that is done for them or to them, and in some cases against them.[23] It is not simply a question of education but of access to the policies of arts institutions and the facilities they control other than as passive consumers. Horne has advocated a declaration of cultural rights, of access to the human cultural heritage, to new art, to community arts participation.

But do artists want that kind of cultural democracy? Danto describes how the Brooklyn Museum has failed its audience and how 'the thirsty millions thirst for art' but what they are searching for is 'an art of their own.'[24] Danto's question, 'public art or the public's art?' encapsulates this nicely. It should be remembered that Glasgow's attempt at a populist, pluralist Gallery of Modern Art celebrating ethnicity, feminism, amateurism – the leitmotifs of postmodernism – has been derided by contemporary art critics and artists despite the fact that a large number of visitors clearly love it, the success of its community outreach schemes, and the fact that the mixing of high and low art is an apparent facet of postmodernism. Art does not lose its responsibility by becoming interesting.

Commodification of culture

One of the legitimate fears of critics and artists about democratisation is that of commodification. Recent research has shown that high art is almost as popular as 'popular' art[25] and the present Government is at pains to dispel what it sees as the 'misleading distinctions' between the two[26] (the same Government source sees itself as the guardian of a creativity that might be 'extinguished' by the formal education system). Importantly, Willis has developed the idea that young people have an alternative, empowering culture based on 'creative consumption.'[27] Much of the fear comes from the arena of fine art as design and architecture are in many senses already commodified, being prey to market forces. Nevertheless, as design critics like Thackara have pointed out, contemporary design has recognised the need to be socially responsible,[28] and Sudjic has described how products from cars to lighters are used to express identity.[29] Designers like Neville Brody are no longer alone in encouraging design to have a more 'critical perspective.'

As a cultural festival Glasgow UK City of Architecture and Design 1999 is a case in point. Certainly, it involves commodification because at one level it is about cultural tourism and, therefore, economic impact. Equally, it is about community participation and education. Indeed, it is those which won the city the accolade. Widening the definition of art to include design, architecture and popular culture ought to go hand in hand with an enlarged view of access and inclusion and should not necessarily see commodification as a barrier. The same goes for making a strengthened case for art education based on the growth of the cultural industries. Some fear that this would be materialist but, such an orientation could go hand in hand with a student-centred curriculum. Both are admissible if the art curriculum is seen as pluralistically as contemporary culture.

Critical culture

This paper has proceeded on the basis that attempts to ameliorate the orthodoxy of the art curriculum in schools – the dichotomy between fine art and design, theory and practice – based on a postmodern reconceptualisation, are potentially flawed because the concept itself is deficient. It has militated against a narrative direction. Proposed instead are a number of postmodernisms of which the post-historical and post-medium are especially useful. One proffers wider cultural possibilities, the other vitiates debates centred on disciplinary content. And, there exists in the form of the GSA Environmental Art course and in the work of its celebrated artist graduates, models, little miracles, new narratives that combine theory and practice and which have embedded context.

The difficulty, however, in advancing an enhanced relationship between school, HE and contemporary art as a way of improving things, was the exclusivity of contemporary art and criticism, especially its language. A grand dialogue was needed rather than a grand narrative, with contemporary artists opening up their work more as suggested by Hewison. Going along with this idea of a more critical culture was the interpolation of the wider creative activities of people, high or low.

Conclusion

If contemporary art and art education really is about process rather than the object then it must involve both audience and artist in the making of meanings. There has to be a grand dialogue, a new receptivity, a new creativity that is not the sole concern of the avant-garde. This is the way to avoid both reactionary modernism and postmodernism. It is only when this critical culture is attained that there will be a secure enough platform to challenge the orthodoxies of school art and find some approximation between the methodologies of secondary and HE. We need new ways of talking, of describing things, of mapping, new themes that integrate and permeate, new forms of research and development. Above all a new direction that does not replace one orthodoxy with another but is a new form of creativity whose context is the entirety of contemporary culture. As William Gibson the science fiction writer once said 'The future has already arrived. It just isn't equally distributed.'

Notes and References

1. MacDonald, S. [1998] Post-it Culture, Postmodernism and Art and Design Education, *Journal of Art & Design Education*, vol 17.3.

2. 'The Death of Art' Danto [1984] was used by the author as a target essay culminating in: Danto, A. [1997] *After the End of Art*. Princeton Academic Press.

3. See for example: Efland, A. et al. [1996] *Postmodern Art Education; An Approach to Curriculum*. Reston Virginia, NAEA.

4. Eagleton, T. [1996] *The Illusions of Postmodernism*. Blackwell.

5. Foster, H. [1996] *The Return of the Real*. Cambridge Mass., MIT Press.

6. See DES [1971] *Art in Schools, Education Survey* 11, HMSO, and SED [19711 *Curriculum Paper 9*. Edinburgh, HMSO.

7. Willis, P. [1990] *Moving Culture*. Calouste Gulbenkian Foundation.

8. Swift, J. [1998] *Time for a Change*, unpublished paper.

9. Harland, J. et al. [1995] *Arts in their View, A Study of Youth Participation in the Arts*. NFER.

10. Rock, M. and Sellars, S. [1998] 'The Museum of the Ordinary,' *EYE, the International Magazine of Graphic Arts*, vol 7.

11. This is a reference to the Schools Council sponsored ABE project – see Adams, E. and Ward, C. [1980] *Art and the Built Environment*. Longman/Schools Council.

12. Rock, M. and Sellars, S. op. cit.

13. Hughes, A. [1998] *Reconceptualising the Art Curriculum*, paper delivered to HMI Seminar.

14. Ibid.

15. Bruner, J. [1996] *The Culture of Education*. Harvard Press.

16. See Gordon-Nesbitt, R. [1998] 'Urban Myths – a tale of two cities' in *Contemporary Visual Arts*, issue 17.

17. See Harding, D. 'Contentious Term and Contested Practice' in Harding, D. and Buckler, I. (eds.) [1998] *Decadence*. Glasgow: Foulis Press.

18. Ainsley, S. [1998] *The Building is Half the Work*, ibid.

19. Esche, C. [1994] 'Escape from the Traps of Art,' Catalogue Essay, *Christine Borland*. Glasgow, Tramway.

20. Kirkpatrick, J. [1996] 'Design as a Tool for Cultural Change' in Verwijnen, J. and Lehtovuori, Y. (eds.) *Managing Urban Change*. University of Art and Design, Helsinki.

21. Mulgan, G. and Warpole, K. [1986] *Saturday Night or Sunday Mornings? From arts to industry – new forms of cultural policy*. Commedia.

22. Hewison, R. [1990] *Future Tense– a new art for the nineties*. Methuen.

23. Horne, D. [1986] *The Public Culture: The Triumph of Industrialism*. Pluto Press.

24. Danto, A. op. cit.

25. Casey, B., Sellwood, S. and Dunlop, R. [1996] *Culture as Commodity: the economics of the arts and the built heritage in the UK*. Policy Studies Institute.

26. Smith, C. [1998] *Creative Britain*. Faber & Faber

27. Willis, P. op. cit.

28. Thackara, J. [1988] *Design After Modernism*. Thames and Hudson.

29. Sudjic, D. [1985] *Cult Objects*. Paladin.

Originally published in the *Journal of Art & Design Education*, volume 18 (1) 1999.

Chapter 6: Postmodern Feminisms: Problematic Paradigms

Lesley Burgess & Diane Reay

Abstract

In 1995 Frances Borzello claimed that feminist art criticism had 'just touched the national curriculum with its fingertips.'[1] Over the last ten years constant challenges to curriculum provision have all but resulted in a loss of contact as educators pull back into 'safe' places and away from the edges where feminist art practices were just starting to take hold. Clinging to 'safe' practices has meant the affirmation of formalist modernist orthodoxies which have fostered a restricted canonical patriarchal approach to the subject. The publication of *A Manifesto for Art in Schools*, 1999 called for a postmodern view of art with an emphasis on 'difference, plurality and independence of mind' can, all too easily, be read as a panacea 'a post modern solution to a postmodern situation.'[2] However, embracing postmodern pluralism creates as many problems as it solves. Postmodernism often renders any feminist intervention superfluous in spite of new feminist art criticisms' insistence that the politics of feminism remains a vital element of both artistic practice and critical discourse. While agreeing that art education urgently needs to review its complicity with high modernist values, we suggest that there are dangers in uncritically accepting a postmodern view of education. Surely postmodernism renders any blueprint for change problematic. This paper does not provide answers, rather it raises questions in order to encourage teachers to reflect upon existing practices with a view to identifying what is still missing and why. It sets out to interrogate implications for pedagogy, educational policy and social transformation of the contemporary academic preoccupation with postmodernism.

Preface

Craig Owens insists that the 'kind of simultaneous activity on multiple fronts that characterises many feminist practices is a postmodern phenomenon.'[3] Janet Wolff, Katy Deepwell, Griselda Pollock and others involved in new feminist art criticism adopt a more sceptical approach.[4]

Postmodernism is an endlessly contestable concept. Few teachers in school have entered into its discourse(s). Similarly it is rare to find a student teacher of art and design who is conversant with its complex and sometimes contradictory positions. Degree courses often encourage art students to engage in postmodern practices without developing the critical understanding needed if they are to articulate a case for its inclusion in the school curriculum. The same can be claimed for postfeminism(s); teachers are aware of the need to move beyond the limited definitions and debates promoted during the 70s – but many are still ill-informed about more recent feminist interventions and readings. Pollock highlights the false dichotomy between past and contemporary 'generations' and calls instead for 'constructed correspondence.' She also reiterates the importance of 'geographies' which are cultural and social as well as political.[5] In line with recent publications by Meskimmon and Perry,[6] Pollock insists that, rather than being passé, the politics of feminism remain a vital element of both artistic practice and intellectual work which is continually reconfigured and reconceptualised in response to who makes it, who curates it, and who reads it.[7]

The way forward?

A Manifesto for Art in Schools bases its proposals on 'a postmodern view of art in education.' The emphasis is on difference, plurality and independence of mind. Knowledge is to be seen as an ever-changing multiplicity of hypotheses or theories, while plurality points to a variety of methods, means, solutions and awareness for any issue. Choice is to be broadened across all forms of art without any implied hierarchy. All this would be fine if all types of knowledge were actually given equal status, but we operate in a social world where knowledge remains rigidly hierarchised.

The recommendations in *A Manifesto for Art in Schools*, that art educators reconceptualise their pedagogic practices and adopt a postmodern curriculum, can on first reading seem like the way forward. However, postmodernism has taught us to question any new constructs in order to identify whether they are in fact offering a new paradigm or are just a wolf in sheep's clothing. Pollock, 1996, reminds us 'difference is far more entangled and complex than we like to admit.'[8]

Within the fields of art production and art education, there are entrenched hierarchies which require critique and questioning rather than (in) difference. As Elizabeth Grosz points out, women are confronted with 'the overwhelming masculinity of historically privileged knowledges.'[9] These privileged knowledges have generated hierarchies of art work in which craft is beneath art, folk art is beneath fine art and activist art is beneath art for art's sake. In the face of such established elitism, attempts to insert minority and women artists retrospectively into a visual art canon constructed by white males have never been sufficient. The prevailing dominance of inclusive perspectives within the art world has meant that even such minor efforts to redress race and gender imbalances are increasingly treated with (in) difference.

It could be argued that women have a much higher profile within contemporary art practice, certainly such figures as Rachel Whiteread and Tracey Emin are as well known as their male counterparts. However, it is important to problematise recent discourses of inclusion and to differentiate between inclusion and equality. Inclusion in a hierarchical field results in an insipid version of equality, one that avoids any recognition of power relations.

In this paper we consider the repercussions of postmodernism for feminist understandings of both art education and production. Postmodernist perspectives have generated postmodern feminisms which we argue are best understood as post feminist rather than feminist conceptions of the social world. If we had anything approaching gender equality, either within the art world or without it, a retreat to apolitical relativism would not be so consequential. However, we also argue that the art world continues to be dominated by 'a male gaze' which needs to be met with a feminist vision rather than the post (feminist) modern 'feminisms' in fashion.

The male artistic legacy

The history of art is a history of the male. Male and man have become conflated with normativity so that we don't even need to specify *male* artist or man's art – all that is needed is the nomenclature art and artist.[10] Before the twentieth century, almost without exception, female artists had been daughters or lovers of famous male artists, while femininity has repeatedly been dissociated from creativity and high culture.[11] As a result, a continual key concern for feminists has been the ways in which white, male, middle class heterosexual values are cultivated and reproduced within the discourses and practices of art. In western culture, art has always been, and remains, an elitist activity, made, and more importantly consecrated by a few, predominantly white males. Jane Gallop argues that postmodernism dephallicizes modernism so men can claim to be new and current. Writing about the literary field, she argues that:

> *If modernism is itself a defence against feminism and the rise of women writers, postmodernism is a more subtle defence, erected when modernism would no longer hold.[12]*

In a dephallicized 'postmodern' art world, 'erected' is perhaps not quite the right word, rather postmodernism constitutes the soft wall hangings and drapes concealing patriarchy's sharper edges.

For Bourdieu:

> *(T)he experience of the work of art as immediately endowed with meaning and value is an effect of the harmony between the two aspects of the same historical institution, the cultivated habitus and the artistic field which mutually ground each other.[13]*

However, the cultivated habitus has historically been a gendered, raced and classed phenomenon premised on the white male gaze. Women arc not only caught up in this male gaze they are also frequently complicit within it, learning how to see themselves and others through the eyes of men.[14] There is a male in even the female head.[15]

The male eye and the (im)possibilities of different ways of looking

> *The moment that one assumes that women are part of humanity in the fullest sense –*
> *the period or set of events with which we deal takes on a wholly different character or*
> *meaning from the normally accepted one. Indeed, what emerges is a fairly regular*
> *pattern of relative loss of status for women in periods of so-called progressive changes.*
> *Suddenly we see these ages with a new double vision and each eye sees a different*
> *picture.[16]*

In the post feminist 2000s we suggest there is not enough double vision; that despite the fashionable plurality of differences and its accompanying fragmentation we are still caught up in a gaze that continues to look with a male eye. Postmodernism, for all its seductive appeal of breaking down hierarchies and celebrating heterogeneity, still maintains the status quo under a different guise.

Beverley Skeggs argues that postmodernism is primarily an attempt by disillusioned male academics, who feel they are no longer at the centre or have authority and control over knowledge, to win back credibility and influence.[17] Joan Hoff, Professor of History at Indiana University, supports such a view, arguing that postmodern theories arise out of a situation that male intellectuals found politically paralysing in post-war Europe, especially in France. As a result French male scholars developed postmodern linguistic theory to rationalise their own disillusionment.[18] Beverley Skeggs (2004) argues that the reality is very different from the postmodernist illusions. Rather, she asserts, in a powerfully classed and gendered analysis, that women, and particularly working-class women, are fixed in place, pinned down by invidious representations that allow their creators, mainly middle-class men, the power to be mobile across social space.[19] If we accept Hoff's and Skeggs' contentions then feminists have good reasons to feel wary about embracing postmodernist insights:

> *… to be postmodern, sociological synthesis must be abandoned for a playful*
> *deconstruction and the privileging of the aesthetic mode.[20]*

It is in this privileging of the aesthetic mode that its seductiveness lies for those of us within the field of art.

However, art education is, and should be, much more than a vehicle for aesthetic experience and both feminists and critical theorists would argue for the importance of continually contextualising art education. Andrea Huyssen questions how there can be any critical discourse in contemporary art programmes if the central curricular issues are restricted to aesthetic experience as the valued end, while all social issues with which works of art deal with are rendered peripheral.[21] Instead, young people should learn to be literate, above all, about those visual documents that explore the conditions and reasons for their social oppression.[22]

Art education's potential as a cultural force in general is rarely linked with the dismantling of oppression in particular. The postmodernist preoccupation with style at the expense of substance compounds already existing tendencies within the art world and results in theories that are elusive and obscure, ungrounded and apolitical.[23] Postmodernism becomes yet another tool of dominance engineered by the powerful in which 'as the marginalised circle modern citadels of power these citadels evanesce into the postmodern mist.'[24]

Seeing through postmodern mists

Beyond the aesthetic, a number of features of postmodernism are deeply problematic for enlightenment projects like feminism that are concerned with rights and empowerment. Perhaps most damaging are postmodernist assertions that there are only fragmentary subjectivities rather than coherent identities. Williams and Bendelow argue that 'not only does art, in its manifold forms, reflect and reinforce dominant beliefs and ideologies within wider society, it is also capable of providing a key site of resistance to prevailing modes of discourse with their normalising assumptions.'[25] However, any emancipatory potential of art is diluted and diffused through postmodernism's fragmentation of the subject. It is deeply problematic to espouse postmodern uncertainty about political categories such as woman or black when the groups making use of these identity categories are only just beginning to make space for themselves historically and culturally within the world of art. The point of postmodernist questioning of subject positions would be for members of dominant groups to acknowledge their biases so that it is possible to recognise the ways in which *their* practices are part of regulatory systems. Instead, feminisms have become infected with an epidemic of radical uncertainty which leaves male hegemony unchallenged.

There are other problematic aspects of postmodernism: it conceptualises power relationships as pluralistic and contingent; it celebrates the surface 'depthlessness' of culture;[26] it gives primacy to eclecticism and the mixing of codes of parody, pastiche, irony and playfulness through stylistic promiscuity. In perverse ways postmodernism is the ideal paradigm for the art world which is what makes it so insidiously dangerous. The postmodern world is opaque, it is all lived on the surface. If there is nothing lurking behind surface appearances then the power imbalances which characterise the art world and the gender positioning and class origins of different artists within the field are irrelevant. They don't mean anything in postmodern accounts. Understanding of historically constructed subjects disappears within a patina of fragmentation and multiplicity. All agency and no structure conspire to make Jill a floating signifier rather than a materially constructed subject, and without an understanding of women as materially constituted subjects feminism as a project has no future either within or without the art field. Individuals who continually create and recreate themselves are not in a position to establish commonalities with others and lose the possibility of describing either common powers of oppression or ways of overcoming them.[27] As a consequence, postmodernism has taken over from modernism as yet another mechanism for repressing feminist agendas. As Seyla Benhabib argues:

> *Postmodernism undermines the feminist commitment to women's agency and sense of selfhood, to the reappropriation of women's own history in the name of an emancipated future, and to the exercise of radical social criticism which uncovers gender 'in all its endless variety and monotonous similarity.'[28]*

Griselda Pollock asserts that art is obsessed with creativity, the creator and *his* creation in ways that posit art as magical, what Bourdieu calls 'the angelic belief in pure interest in a pure form.' (Bourdieu 1996: xiv)[29] In contrast, Pollock argues that new epistemologies, which facilitate a focus on the continuities within the art world, are needed; epistemologies which allow us to gain a sense of what has remained the same despite contemporary emphases on plurality, diversity and fragmentation. She also utilises hegemonic understandings of femininity and masculinity in order to sketch out a dialectical relationship in which women's art is conflated with femininity which in turn is conflated with mediocre art. Working with very different notions of difference to those in postmodern feminisms she conceptualises femininity as operating as a degraded difference against which an unacknowledged masculine superiority can be maintained.[30]

Postmodernist influences are increasingly evident in contemporary art production, particularly in the wave of apoliticism and indifference to wider social issues. Contemporary art may appear to have eschewed the elitism of its modernist tradition but it also eschews social critique and theory. Instead we have:

> *casual, promiscuous, populist art which wishes to be repositioned within the chat-show world of celebrity culture, alongside the sponsorship deals, inside the restaurants and at the very heart of consumer culture.[31]*

While the brashness, irreverence and populism of the work of artists like Sarah Lucas and Damien Hirst clearly challenges the pretentiousness and snobbery of the art world, it also adamantly refuses the role of social criticism. For example, for Sarah Lucas 'the sex thing, the way men look at women, I'm not so bothered about these days. I find it funny more than anything else.'[32] We suggest that modern artists could do with getting angry rather than getting playful. As Angie McRobbie contends, Emin's tent 'owes more to the "girls just wanna have fun" humour of *More* magazine than it does to her feminist elders, Cindy Sherman or Mary Kelly.'[33]

Postmodern feminisms: Problematic paradigms or contradiction in terms?

Postmodernism and feminism are uncomfortable bedfellows. Politically aware work and research is either seen as dangerous or naive within postmodern feminisms, while highlighting gender inequalities discomforts many successful postmodern feminists who have reached a rapprochement with patriarchal systems and the men who run them. Somer Brodribb[34] argues that, because postmodern feminisms are an arrangement with, and selection from, male theory rather than female experience, the only identity politics in postmodern feminisms is identification with male texts. While feminisms have always been grounded in oppositional stances, postmodern tactics of pastiche, irony and playfulness skirt around any oppositional stance, avoiding the possibilities of challenge in attempts to subvert or reappropriate. An argument can be made that postmodern feminisms constitute more than problematic paradigms. To the extent that postmodernism swallows up and engulfs feminisms; co-opting and silencing feminist interpretations and readings, it can be seen to be a contradiction in terms. Postmodernism in the field of art has encouraged an anarchic liberalism which suspends judgment in the name of pluralism. It masquerades under the guise of dismantling hierarchies whilst remaining blind to already existing hierarchies which are as entrenched as ever both within and without the world of art. As Hawthorne asserts, 'Postmodernism is a masculine theory that posits difference as a foil to its own indifference.'[35]

Conclusion

Feminism is a broad umbrella term: it allows the inclusion of a diverse, eclectic, range of work. It welcomes contradictions, inconsistencies and incoherence, all those aspects reviled and rejected by phallocentric logic. It is old enough to have its own history(ies), art historians, critics, and, although ostensibly it refutes objectification, it has established its own 'series of academically marked objects' against which new works are considered. If this is the case then art educators need to acknowledge it. Through social reproduction and cultural capital, formal and informal education teachers and their students have been introduced to the legitimised discourse of the western canon – a list of OK male artists. Bourdieu insists that it is important to acknowledge that education is a powerful means of social reproduction and recognise what he refers to as 'symbolic violence,' that is the imposition of systems and meaning (i.e., culture) upon groups (or classes) in such a way that they are experienced as legitimate.[36]

The 'Manifesto' insists 'reconsideration is needed if the education and development of teachers is to provide the essential theoretical and philosophical underpinning needed to sustain them in practice.'[37] We suggest that the underpinning needed is one that includes a critical evaluation of deeply embedded, existing hierarchies of knowledge within both the world of art production and the world of education. To ensure that this 'essential … underpinning' is not just essentially male, teachers need to be cognisant of the fact that, for at least the last forty years, there has been a powerful feminist impact on art production. This contribution needs to be introduced to our students in its complexity and diversity recognising its impact on contemporary practice. Postmodernism has tended to neutralise such practices, consequently men adopt feminist positions and claim them as their own.

Independent thought is recognised as essential in the 'Manifesto.' Wolff (1990) reminds us:

> *Women's work … is given considerably less space in critical discussion. … and historical establishments for the most part remain resistant to feminist work and to the necessary reconceptualisation of the history and practice of the arts.*[38]

Meecham reiterates this by claiming that the National Curriculum has given limited recognition to the challenge presented by feminism:

> *… it does nothing to undo the structures that hold in place received opinion which argues that women's art is derivative and not innovative enough to gain a place in the canon defined in a masculine culture – … a hard paradigm to shift.'*[39]

We must avoid the notion that we are free agents (or free thinkers), that in art education we can escape the 'legitimising discourse' (symbolic violence) that insists we stay in line – perpetuating preconditioned responses which are powerfully conditioned by dominant social discourses which still sees men as more powerful. Postmodernism has to be approached with scepticism, recognised as redolent with possibilities – but also open to limited interpretation. Jameson suggested Van Gogh's *Peasant Boots* provides a key example of modernism while David Hockney's *Diamond Dust Shoes* epitomises postmodernism.[40] We are in danger of replacing one set of men's shoes for another. If we are to deconstruct the father's house (modernism) we need to be aware that we can't do it using the father's tools.

With postmodernism do women have a voice? Or have they been written into a male discourse only to find themselves on the outside looking in on their inclusion, subsumed yet still peripheral?

Notes and References

1. Borzello, F. in Deepwell, K (ed.) [1995] *New Feminist Art Criticism*. Manchester University Press, p. 22.

2. Swift, J. & Steers, J. [1999] *Manifesto for Art in Schools*, JADE 18.1.

3. Owens, C. [1985] *Discourses of Others: Feminist and Postmodernism*.

4. Wolff, J. [1990] *Feminine Sentences: Essays on Women & Culture*. Polity Press, Cambridge; Deepwell, K (ed.) [1995] *New Feminist Art Criticism*, Manchester University Press; Pollock, G. (ed.) [1996] *Generations and Geographies in the Visual Arts: Feminist Readings*, London: Routledge.

5. Pollock, G. (ed.) [1996] ibid.

6. Meskimmon, M. [2003] *Women Making Art: History Subjectivity and Aesthetics* London: Routledge; Perry, G. (ed.) [2004] *Difference and Excess in Contemporary Art: The Visibility of Women's Practice*, Oxford: Blackwell.

7. Pollock, G. (ed.) [1996] ibid.

8. Pollock, G. [1996] *Into the Visible*, MAKE 71, p. 25.

9. Grosz, E. [1995] *Space, Time and Perversion*. London: Routledge, p. 45.

10. Pollock, G. [1988] *Vision and Difference: Femininity, feminism and histories of art*. London: Routledge.

11. Nochlin, L. [1973] 'Why have there been no great women artists' in Hess T. and Baker, E. (eds.) *Art and Sexual Politics*. Harmondsworth: Penguin.

12. Gallop, J. [1988] *Thinking through the Body*. New York: Columbia University Press, p. 100.

13. Bourdieu, P. [1996] *The Rules of Art*. Cambridge: Polity Press. p. 289.

14. Holland, J. et al. [1998] *The Male in the Head: Young people, heterosexuality and power*. London: The Tufnell Press.

15. Holland, J., Sharpe, S., Ramazanoglu, C. and Thomson, R. [1998] *The Male in the Head*. London, Tufnell Press.

16. Gadol, J. [1984] 'The Social Relations of the Sexes: Methodological Implications of Women's History' in *Women, History and Theory*. Chicago: University of Chicago Press, pp. 1–14.

17. Skeggs, B. [1991] 'Postmodernism: What's all the fuss?' *British Journal of Sociology of Education*, vol 12, no 2, pp. 255–267.

18. Hoff, J. [1994] 'Gender as a Post-Modern Category of Paralysis' *Women's Studies International Forum* 17 (4), pp. 443–447.

19. Skeggs, B [2004] *Class, Self, Culture London*. Routledge; London

20. Skeggs B. [1991] Postmodernism: What's all the fuss? *British Journal of Sociology of Education*, vol 12, no 2, p. 257.

21. Huyssen, A. [1990] 'Mapping the Postmodern' in Linda Nicholson (ed.) *Feminism/Postmodernism*. London: Routledge.

22. Lanier, V. [1980] 'Six items on the agenda for the eighties,' *Art Education* 33 (1), pp. 16–23.

23. Fehr, D. [1993] *Dogs playing cards: Powerbrokers of Prejudice in Education, Art and Culture*. New York: Peter Lang Publishing.

24. Ibid. p. 81.

25. Williams, S. & Bendelow, G. [1998] *The Lived Body: Sociological Themes, Embodied Issues*. London: Routledge, p. 193.

26. Featherstone, M. [1988] in *Postmodernism, Theory, Culture and Society*. London: Sage.

27. Assiter, A. [1996] *Enlightened Women: Modernist Feminism in a Postmodern Age*. London: Routledge.

28. Benabib, S. [1992] *Situating the Self: Gender, Community and Postmodernism in Contemporary Ethics*, Cambridge: Polity Press, p. 229.

29. Bourdieu [1996]: xiv.

30. Pollock, *Generations & Geographies*.

31. McRobbie, A. [1998] 'But is it Art?' *Marxism Today* Nov/Dec.

32. Lucas, S. quoted in *The Sunday Times*, 8/11/98.

33. McRobbie, A. [1998] 'But is it Art?' *Marxism Today* Nov/Dec 1998 p. 55.

34. Brodribb, S. [1992] *Nothing Mat(t)ers: A Feminist Critique of Post-Modernism*. New York: New York University Press.

35. Hawthorne, S. [1996] 'From Theories of Indifference to a Wild Politics' in *Radically Speaking: Feminism Reclaimed* (eds.) Diane Bell and Renate Klein. London: Zed Books, p. 486.

36. Jenkins, R. [1992] *Pierre Bourdieu*. London: Routledge, p. 104.

37. Swift, J. & Steers, J. [1999] *Manifesto for Art in Schools*, JADE 18.1.

38. Wolff, J. [1990] *Feminine Sentences: Essays on Women & Culture*. Polity Press Cambridge, p. 73.

39. Meecham, P. [1996] 'What is a National Curriculum?' in Dawtrey et al. *Critical Studies & Art Education*. OU press, Milton Keynes, p. 74.

40. Jameson, F. 'Postmodernism and Consumer Society' in Foster, H. [1991] *The Anti -Aesthetic: Essays on Modern Culture*, pp. 111–125.

Originally published in the *Journal of Art & Design Education*, volume 18 (3) 1999.

Chapter 7: The Knowing Body: Art as an Integrative System of Knowledge

John Danvers

Overview

Drawing upon research in a number of fields (particularly in ecology, 'systems' approaches to perception, the philosophy of science, and the phenomenology of Merleau-Ponty and his interpreters) this paper raises issues and questions about the relationships between knowledge, art and science. It suggests a way of thinking about art as an integrative system of knowledge based upon the recognition of three important factors: our fundamental participation in the world as knowing bodies; the perspectival nature of our interpretations of the world; and the particular ways in which we achieve coherence and integration through the making of art. The paper also traces some of the changes in the ways in which knowledge is described and formulated within modernist and postmodernist paradigms, and suggests how these changes support a revision of our views about the cognitive implications of art.

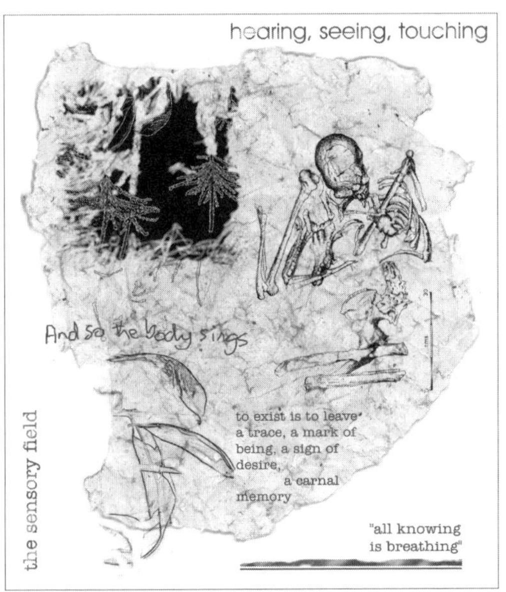

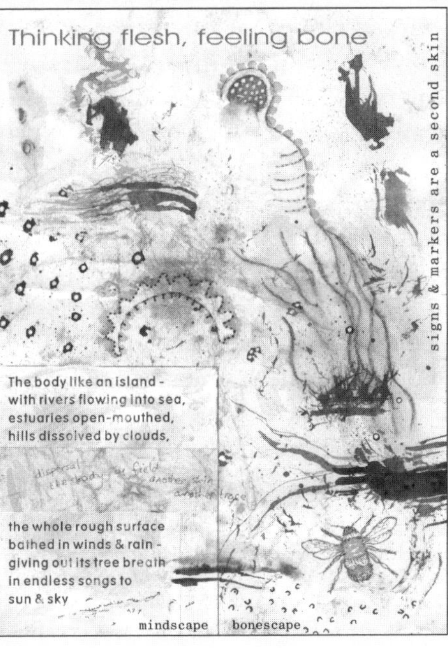

Sensory Field 2 *and* Second Skin 3 *from 'Pictograph series' 2004 by John Danvers*

Scientists do not deal with truth … they deal with limited and approximate descriptions of reality. Capra, F. [1992] Belonging to the Universe. Penguin

Introduction

Many contemporary scientists and philosophers of science argue that science is not so much about constructing theories which progressively reveal the 'true nature of things,' but is rather about formulating 'limited and approximate descriptions' of the events, processes and systems which constitute reality.

This suggests a convergence between science and art – in the sense that artistic production, in many cases, can be seen as an attempt, through analysis, invention, reformulation and synthesis, to construct 'approximate descriptions' of reality.

My intention in this paper is to explore some of the ways in which such descriptions are formulated, and to relate this process to the wider question of how we should think about knowledge and perception. My aim is to raise issues and questions rather than to formulate a linear argument. I will be drawing upon research in a number of fields – particularly in ecology, systems theory, the philosophy of science, and the phenomenology of Merleau-Ponty and his interpreters.

The visual arts as forms of knowledge

It could be argued that too much emphasis has been placed upon the visual arts as forms of 'self-expression,' and that this emphasis has led to a neglect of the wider functions and significance of the visual arts, both in cultural and educational terms. I'm thinking here of the expressive theories promulgated by Collingwood and Worringer, and the expressive aesthetics exemplified in the ideas and practices of artists such as Klee, Kandinsky, Munch and Pollock. At the centre of expressive aesthetics lies the belief that the purpose of art is to express emotion as directly as possible, to transfer emotional feeling in all its purity and intensity from artist to audience via the artwork. Whether this is possible and how we could know if the expressive transfer had taken place are questions that immediately arise. Although this is not the place to explore these issues, we can note that despite the centrality of expressive aesthetics to modernist practices and the subjectivist legacy they bequeath to contemporary culture, such theories and practices are problematic and should not be left unchallenged.

Although the visual arts do undoubtedly have a role to play in the expression of feeling, many expressive theories tend both to neglect other means of representing feelings and emotions, and also tend to confirm the preconceptions of many academics that the visual arts are marginal to the mainstream of education.

In order to counteract the distortions brought about by this situation the visual arts should be considered as forms of knowledge (and artists as formulators of knowledge) alongside literature, science, music and philosophy. This provides a more inclusive way of categorising and thinking about art and, at the same time, a return to a way of describing the visual arts prevalent prior to the early decades of the 20th century.

In earlier centuries artists were seen as contributing to the whole spectrum of human knowledge by picturing human and non-human spheres of existence in iconic, indexical and symbolic images. Artists produced visual and spatial images and narratives that were modes of analysing and describing the world – showing us different aspects of the world, how human beings are in the world, what we do and how we think and feel about ourselves and the world about us. The obsession with expressing emotion that characterised much of the art produced from late eighteenth century romanticism, through to the many forms of twentieth century expressionism, was closely associated with the development of modernism and its excessive emphasis on subjectivism, individualism and the almost pathological cult of 'genius.' This narrowing of the parameters of artistic activity (at least within the avant-garde echelons of 'high-art') was both extreme and relatively short-lived. Since the 1960s, the expressive/self-expressive aesthetic, although still operational (particularly in popular perceptions of art and the artist), has become only one of many ideas, methods and practices that compete within the cultures of postmodernism.

What do we mean by knowing and knowledge?

The terms know and knowledge have a complex etymological history. Two distinct roots can be traced: 'to know by the senses'; and 'to know by the mind' – from which at least three meanings developed:

- Firstly – to recognise; to identify … to be able to distinguish (one thing) from (another),
- Secondly – to be acquainted with (a thing, a place or person); to be familiar with; to have personal experience of (something), and,
- Thirdly – to learn through observation, information or inquiry … to find out … to be conversant with through study or practice … to acquire skill in; to have a clear or distinct perception of … Knowledge while referring to the above usages also refers to 'a branch of learning; a science; an art.'

It is self-evident that these definitions accurately describe many of the diverse functions of drawing, painting, sculpture or other visual constructs, and suggest a much more comprehensive view of their significance.

Being, knowing and embodiment

These commonly accepted definitions and usages are couched in very general terms, however, we need to establish a more precise conceptual framework within which our understanding of knowledge can be located, shedding light on the processes by which we gain knowledge in everyday experience and through the making of, and engagement with, the visual arts.

At the outset we have to establish a location for the processes of coming to knowledge – an existential and physiological context without which knowledge, consciousness and being are mere abstractions.

If we are not to perpetuate the mind/body dualism which has characterised and bedevilled Western philosophy for many centuries, indeed if we are not to amputate the mind from the body, we have to begin by recognising that the primary site of each mind is a particular finite corporeal body. A secondary site could be identified in the form of the many constructs, messages and markers which the mind/body externalises and presents to others – all human production could be said to constitute this secondary site – a body outside – a shadow of the primary site. This corporeal body is the locus of the mind's operations, providing its sustenance, systemic foundation and contact with the world. The concept of the disembodied subject/mind reduces the subject/mind to a fantasy, a rather implausible ghost or abstraction.

This paper therefore assumes a holistic view of an embodied subject/mind in interrelationship with other embodied subjects. It assumes that though we can speak of the mind and body as separate entities, we ought never to make the mistake of believing they are anything other than integrated systems, operationally active only together, mutually sustaining, validating and energising.

It follows that philosophically we need to stress the way in which epistemology and ontology are interwoven, that our knowledge is acquired through our being-in-the-world, or as Paul Crowther writes, describing Merleau-Ponty's view, 'our knowledge of the world is gained through our body's exploration of the world.'[1]

Kierkegaard probably had a similar attitude but presented it in a typically aphoristic (and cryptic) remark: 'all knowledge is breathing.'[2]

The knowing body

Knowledge is rooted in our needs and intentions, and in our responses to the situations in which we find ourselves. As we negotiate and learn to 'handle' the world we assimilate and construct a 'body of knowledge' which informs our attitudes and actions. The primary site of knowledge is within the purposive consciousness which inhabits, or, more correctly, is embodied as a particular physiological entity (my body: your body). Knowledge is externalised in a secondary site comprising the products of human learning – the 'constructs, messages and markers' referred to earlier. Included in this externalisation are the bodies of knowledge which constitute the visual arts – paintings, sculpture, films, photographs, installations and performances.

Knowledge can be described as referring to two or three spheres of experience:

- knowledge of the world;
- knowledge of oneself; and
- knowledge of a transcendent, transpersonal or ultimate reality – God or the Ground of Being in Christian mysticism, Brahman in Hinduism, or sunyata in Buddhist terminology.

The latter category perhaps having meaning for only a minority in our secular and materialistic Western culture, but certainly of great importance to many in the past and from other cultures.

The maxim of Aristotle that, 'there is nothing in the mind that was not first in the senses',[3] bears witness to the longevity of the view that all knowledge, ultimately, is afforded by the mediation of the senses – the embodiment of perception. However, it could be argued that a number of distinct categories of experience are involved, each qualitatively different to the others. For example:

- the senses (perception);
- the mind (rational and discursive thought);
- the 'spirit' ('the eye with which we look at God, and the eye with which God looks at us') – all of which are integrated, unified and interdependent.

'Intuition' could be placed in either, or both, of the mind or spirit categories dependent upon the conceptual and cultural frameworks being applied.

Coming to know – the senses

We come to know about the world through our perceptions of it – through the 'butterfly net of the senses.' This process can be described either with reference to the classical five senses (sight, touch, hearing, taste, smell) or to the more sophisticated models proposed over the past twenty to thirty years by perceptual psychologists and neurologists. James Gibson suggests a model in which the senses are described as five perceptual systems:[4]

- Basic orienting system: the inner ear – specifying the direction of gravity and the beginning and ending of body movement;
- Auditory system: vibrations of air on the ear drum, specifying the nature and direction of auditory events;
- Haptic system: receptors in tissues and joints, specifying posture and movements of limbs and muscles, and touch at the surface of the skin;

- Olfactory system: taste and smell working together;
- Visual system: specifying the structure of ambient light.

All these systems overlap and interact to provide as much information as possible. Gibson stresses that this is an information-based network, rather than sensation-based. Pliny, writing in the 1st Century AD, would no doubt have agreed with him, for he describes 'the mind as the real instrument of sight and observation.'[5] The senses provide information to the brain which is already partially ordered, selected and 'interpreted' – rather than indecipherable masses of 'raw' sensory data. The basic orienting system and the haptic system are particularly important in proprioception – the body's awareness of itself, while the auditory, olfactory and visual systems are important in exteroception – awareness of the external environment.

It is important to note that even in Gibson's systems view of perception there is a tendency to separate the perceiving subject from the objects of perception. The perceptual systems are viewed as interactive and interdependent but the relationship between these embodied systems and the ambient world appears estranged. Gibson stresses the need to consider the senses as active interdependent systems of enquiry, concerned with finding out, investigating, exploring, sorting and making sense.

Bronowski writes:

> *The world is not a fixed, solid array of objects, out there, for it cannot be fully separated from our perception of it. It shifts under our gaze, it interacts with us, and the knowledge that it yields has to be interpreted by us.*[6]

Merleau-Ponty argues that our

> *… fundamental contact with things arises from a practical synthesis – from our handling them, looking at them, using them.*[7]

Paul Crowther summarises Merleau-Ponty's, theory of perception in the following terms:

> *The body articulates the world into meanings by grasping it through the integrated operation of the senses, and relating what is thus grasped to its past and future life. In this sense perception is creative.*[8]

The neurologists Maturana and Varela state that, 'every act of knowing brings forth a world.' They add, 'All doing is knowing, and all knowing is doing'[9] – emphasising that knowing is an activity, a process, a participation, an encounter, a relating to.

The dividing line between perceptual activity and mental activity is shifting and ill-defined, and the subject of much scientific debate. However, it does seem that perception itself has selecting, categorising and unifying functions. Analysis, evaluation and synthesis appear to take place to some extent at the origin of input. The mind and its functions represent further levels of refinement and interpretation of perceptual information, and new stages of evaluation, decision-making and storage. Perception, memory, thinking and doing all contribute to the prospective and speculative activity of coming to know the world – exemplified in the arts as well as the sciences.

Similarly these factors are all utilised in knowing oneself – but it is important to remember that the classical senses must be extended to include proprioceptive systems such as the haptic and basic orienting systems.

Coming to know God or acquiring knowledge of a reality immanent within, or beyond, the 'veil of appearances' which is our everyday reality, is a process too complex and contentious to enter into here – but suffice it to say that many would argue that it is possible – once more through the medium of the senses and the powers of the mind, coupled with divine grace, faith and a contemplative giving-up or dissolution of the ego (to use Christian terminology).

Subject and object as unified system or field

If we examine the writings of phenomenologists (particularly Merleau-Ponty), Gestalt theorists, psychologists of perception like James Gibson, philosophers of science like Kuhn and Capra, and a number of Buddhist thinkers some similar attitudes are evident. For instance:

- an emphasis upon a holistic 'systems' view;
- a stress upon the interactive interdependence of subject and object; and
- an emphasis upon process.

When we look at perception we can see how these attitudes affect understanding of the relationship between subject and object, perceiver and perceived. While Gibson formulates a systems view based upon five perceptual systems, we could go further and argue that the primary system involved is that which integrates subject and object, observer and observed – the energised, activated relationship between perceiver and perceived needs to be considered as the primary system. We can divide this systemic relationship into 'subject' and 'object,' 'me' and 'the world,' but in reality they are indivisible.

Perception, mind and consciousness are functions of the interaction and fluctuating tension between body and world – in a sense they are the 'skin,' the surface belonging as much to the environment as to the individual. Just as quantum physics illuminates the interactive processes between apparently separate subatomic particles or events – teaching us that the distinctions and divisions we make are to some extent arbitrary and always conditional – so the experience of perception, of coming-to-know our world, also presents us with the basic features of interconnection and indivisibility.

David Bohm, the quantum physicist, writes:

> *We suggest that there is indeed a meaning to a reality that lies outside ourselves but that it is necessary that we, too, should be included in an essential way as participants in this reality. Our knowledge of the universe is derived from this act of participation.*[10]

The observer is always part of the observation. To put this another way: I look out at the world through a part of the world. The world looks at a part of itself. I am part of the world's perception of itself. Or: we gain knowledge of the world, of what is, through our implication in the world, through our assimilation into the world. In a sense we are the consciousness of the world, of what is.

Knowledge and networks

Capra and others have pointed to the 'network' as an important diagrammatic icon of the new thinking in science; it is also significant in relation to our understanding of knowledge and the visual arts. Capra writes:

> *As we perceive reality as a network of relationships, our descriptions, too, form an interconnected network representing the observed phenomena. In such a network there will be neither hierarchies nor foundations.*[11]

This sounds like a prospectus for postmodernism! The network, as a whole, constitutes a multifaceted, multivalent and ever-changing body of learning, description and interpretation. Any part of it, taken in isolation (be it scientific theory or body of artworks), provides a limited and approximate viewpoint – which is all any of us (individual, group, institution or class), can propose. The notion of some kind of objective certainty, or of a holy grail of ultimate truth, sought by many and found by only a privileged few, can be seen as a potentially dangerous misconception, or an irrelevant fantasy.

Achieving coherence and making sense

All knowing involves the utilisation of processes of selection, evaluation, analysis and synthesis. It is obvious that these characteristics of coming-to-know, of ordering and making sense, of 'achieving coherence,' are as typical of the arts as of the sciences. And while music may be questioned as a way of 'knowing about the world' this is no more debatable than the case of pure mathematics. Both certainly generate constructs which model or represent states of coherence or relative incoherence. And in the case of music many have argued that it also models in a programmatic or impressionistic manner states of mind. Liebniz suggests a provocative analogy between numbers and music: 'The pleasure we obtain from music comes from counting, but counting unconsciously. Music is nothing but unconscious arithmetic.'[12]

All knowing also involves the construction of propositions, models and schema which are functionally related to our activities in the world, and which are in a continuous process of modification and revision. The repository of propositions and models which is a culture, is only a reflection of that repository of propositions and models which is an individual mind.

The organisation of material into a pictorial construct or system of visual signs (for instance, a painting or sculpture) is analogous to the process of ordering sensations and experience through the perceptual systems and the mind. There is also a close analogy between the process of making a visual construct and a view of learning as a self-transcendent project fundamental to life. Capra relates learning to biological development and evolution:

> *Living organisms have an inherent potential for reaching out beyond themselves to create new structures and new patterns of behaviour. This creative reaching out into novelty, which in time leads to an ordered unfolding of complexity, seems to be a fundamental property of life.[13]*

The speculative nature of learning, taking risks in order to enter new states of knowledge, is also a primary feature of the making of art – both in relation to the minutiae of handling materials, (for instance: modulating colour across a surface; modelling a form in clay; or finding the 'right' marks for a passage of drawing), and in relation to the development of ideas or a philosophy of practice.

The cognitive, perceptual, affective and performative qualities required to make a coherent and significant visual construct, are as profound, as diverse and as subtle, as those required in any other branch of learning.

What kinds of knowledge do we find embodied in visual constructs?

If the visual arts constitute bodies of knowledge, what kinds of knowledge do we find in them? A brief list may indicate some of the variety and scope evident in even a cursory examination (these fields of knowledge are not mutually exclusive and are likely to coexist in the work of a particular artist).

Specific sensory information about the visible world

Artists provide sensory information about the visible world in terms of colour, tonal values, surface texture, qualities of light and atmosphere. For example, Constable's empirical approach, encapsulated in his well-known statement that:

86 Art Education in a Postmodern World: Collected Essays

Painting is a science, and should be pursued as an inquiry into the laws of nature. Why, then, may not landscape painting be considered as a branch of natural philosophy, of which pictures are but the experiments?[14]

Eugene Fromentin, writing about Jacob Ruisdael, describes the way in which Ruisdael gathers and represents information about the natural world, especially the sky: 'He curves and spreads it, measures it, determines its value in relation to the variations of light on the terrestrial horizon.' Fromentin also mentions Ruisdael's 'circular field of vision,' the painter's 'grand eye open to everything that lives.'[15]

Svetlana Alpers writes of Dutch painting in the 17th Century:

The aim of Dutch painters was to capture on a surface a great range of knowledge and information about the world. They too employed words with their images. Like the mappers, they made additive works that could not be taken in from a single viewing point. Theirs was not a window on the Italian model of art but rather, like a map, a surface on which is laid out an assemblage of the world.[16]

Specific structural information about the visible world

This kind of knowledge is the product of analytical enquiry and observation, and is concerned with understanding the patterns and structures which underpin the world of appearances. Work in this category tends to present us with systems and essences and is concerned with taxonomy as much as description. For instance, the mathematical, geological and anatomical knowledge developed and stored in landscape and figure paintings, sculptures and drawings from the late 15th century onwards. The anatomical drawings of Leonardo, and Stubbs' drawings and paintings of horses are obvious examples, but a comprehensive listing would be vast and would have to include the work of Cezanne and the earlier work of Mondrian, as well as sculptors as varied as Michelangelo and Degas.

Ruskin expressed a view similar to Constable's notion of art as 'a branch of natural philosophy,' however he encouraged artists to develop an acuity of perception which would identify the inner structural properties of the natural world, rather than the surface detail.[17]

Systematic two-dimensional models of three-dimensional space

Knowledge of this kind includes the countless forms of perspective and projective systems (Eastern and Western), and the modelling of solids. The visual arts share this epistemological territory with mathematics and geometry. The ideas and drawings of Piero della Francesca and Brunelleschi can be considered alongside Pythagorus and Euclid as ways of formulating systematic diagrammatic models of three-dimensional space.

Three-dimensional analyses of the interaction between volumes, materials and mass in space

Although the European traditions of sculpture between the gothic and modern periods seem predisposed to descriptive realism (which places more emphasis upon ocular veracity than tactile truth), all sculpture to some extent models the operation and experience of the haptic and basic orienting systems, affirming our experience of corporeal weight within a gravitational field – a celebration and analysis of embodiment. Examples include works as varied as Michelangelo's *David*, Rodin's *Burgher's of Calais*, de Kooning's *Clam Digger*, Caro's *Early One Morning*, Rachel Whiteread's *House*, as well as ancestor stools produced in Ghana and Inuit shamanic masks.

Representations of 'subjective' human experience

Knowledge acquired through reflection and speculation about what it feels like to be a certain person in a certain place at a certain time – encompassing psychological, existential and spiritual domains. This includes ontological knowledge encoded, enacted and interrogated in a huge variety of works produced by artists as dissimilar as Rembrandt (the self-portraits), Van Gogh, Francis Bacon, Bill Viola, Frank Auerbach, Giacometti, Helen Chadwick or Cindy Sherman.

Representations of what might be the case, what might happen or has happened

The speculative domain of the imagination – of visual fictions, fables, prophecy and historical reconstruction. Examples range from the work of Titian, Rubens and Blake to Dalí, Joel Peter Witkin, Clifford Possum Tjapaltjarri and Paula Reago.

The latter two categories tend to present knowledge of ourselves in the world, as against knowledge of the world itself.

Presentations of the thing-in-itself or 'objecthood'

There is also a category of art production characterised by its explicitly non-representational intent. The work of artists who aim to assert the 'objectness' of the object, the 'presence' of the concrete, material substance of the world. The 'art of the real' – as manifested in certain minimalist/process artists. This could be seen as constituting an attempt to generate situations in which we gain unmediated direct knowledge of the world, of what is – though many would argue that this is impossible. Examples include 'minimalist' works produced by Don Judd, Richard Serra, Carl Andre. The sacred Kaaba in Mecca could be seen as another example within the non-representational framework of Islamic art. The famous Japanese temple rock garden of Daitokuji or the one-stroke ink drawings of Nantembo, can also be seen as a manifestation of tathata or 'suchness,' a showing of 'that which is' within a Buddhist context.

Art and science: concrete and abstract

Of course the visual arts, in the main, present knowledge in concrete forms (indices of the body and its operations), through physically insistent materials and processes, which are themselves functionally linked to maker, and the processes of manufacture. The knowledge developed by the unified, interactive field of body/mind/environment is itself 'embodied' in artefacts and processes which are themselves part of the interactive networks which constitute their context, site and audience – a system or field of relationships.

Although this paper has assumed a high degree of congruence between the visual arts and the sciences it is worth considering one or two points of potential difference.

Science aims at a level of abstraction in its knowledge, a position in which generalisations are possible, beyond and above the level of specific cases. Science aims in some way towards theories which are applicable, if not universally, then at least to as wide a range of cases and situations as possible. The tendency (the danger if you like) is towards disembodied knowledge, whereas we could say (in polarising the possibilities) that the tendency in the visual arts is towards 'over-embodied' knowledge, that is hyperspecificity. A situation in which knowledge obtains or is present only in that particular object/situation/case, and has no applicability, relevance or even accessibility to other individuals or situations. This is a kind of extreme subjectivity in which highly subjective 'content' has, and can have, no cognitive significance to anyone else, perhaps because it is encoded and enclosed in an arcane or private field of gravity, which, like a black hole, might draw in but not radiate energy (in this case illumination or knowledge). Of course this degree of collapsing or imploding subjectivity could be considered as an absence of any cognitive dimension at all, on the basis that knowledge which can only be 'known' by one person (the artist/maker), cannot by definition be verified or recognised as knowledge by anyone else. This would constitute a closed system – which many would argue is the case with some kinds of artefacts and processes, which deny access by virtue of their hyper-subjectivity.

Knowledge, modernism and postmodernism

The way in which knowledge is described, categorised and formulated has changed radically over the past century. Most recently this shift can be seen in terms of the modernist/postmodernist divide.

Increasingly our study of knowledge is feeling the impact of holistic, systems-based thinking evident in the sciences, and increasingly in the arts. Modes of organisation, process and relationship have become the focus of attention and enquiry. Fields of energy, indeterminacy, dynamic interaction and interdependence are now emphasised and valued, while the more deterministic emphasis upon establishing laws and certainties governing inert solids and substances has been questioned and found to be unsatisfactory. The paradigm shift (if that is what it is) from a Newtonian mechanistic, atomistic worldview, to a worldview grounded in systems and process thinking, is evident in the ways in which we engage with knowledge, and in the cultural morphology of postmodernism.

This shift in the way knowledge and learning are viewed, constitutes a move from a kind of epistemological absolutism to one of contingency and relativity. In the former there is a relatively clear sense of what is established, fixed, orthodox, and, by implication, true, as regards bodies of knowledge and the objects of knowledge. In the new scenario contingency, approximation and limitation are seen as necessary conditions of any viewpoint or position. No single position can be seen as holding a monopoly of truth, indeed diverse and multiple viewpoints are affirmed and valued.

The modernist approach can be described as being essentially linear and oriented about a vertical axis. Emphasis is placed upon achieving understanding through a progressive development which is essentially teleological and compartmentalised. There is a movement towards an accretive accumulation of information and knowledge.

On the other hand the postmodernist approach tends to be non-linear, or multi-linear, oriented about a lateral axis, emphasising connection, relationship, interdependence and complexity. The web of energies and relationships which characterises the world of nature is reflected in the multifaceted and perspectival character of human understanding. Knowledge is always conditioned by the location, purpose and outlook of the knowing subject. The process of knowing is essentially interpretative, never absolute.

Summing up

In this survey of some of the issues and ideas about knowledge, interpretation and the visual arts I have suggested that the cognitive function of art parallels that of the sciences. I identified some of the ways in which the visual arts present us with embodiments of knowledge in the form of processes and artefacts. We have seen how this knowledge is the product of human participation in the world through the medium of the body and its processes. We also recognised how knowledge is inherently perspectival, an interpretation arising from our participation in the world. This acknowledgement of the interpretative basis of our knowledge, embodied in artefacts and processes, led us to recognise the importance of integration and coherence in the way we make sense of the world and in the way we make art. Finally we have seen, I hope, how the integrative coherence of the models, constructs and processes manifested in the visual arts promotes a re-integration in the observer – a reformulation of experience, a re-interpretation of what is. Perhaps we can also see the way in which all observers, that is all of us, are participants, spiders if you like, spinning the web of interpretations which constitutes culture.

Notes and References

1. Crowther, P. [1993] *Critical Aesthetics and Postmodemism*. Oxford University Press.

2. Jolivet, R. [1950] *Introduction to Kierkegaard*. Frederick Muller.

3. Quoted by Roger Bacon in *De Intellectu et Intelligentia*, c. 1270.

4. Gibson, J. J. [1968] *The Senses Considered as Perceptual Systems*. Allen and Unwin.

5. Gombrich, E. H. [1977] *Art and Illusion*. Phaidon Press.

6. Bronowski, J. [1988] *The Ascent of Man*. BBC Publications.

7. Crowther, P. op. cit.

8. Ibid.

9. Maturana, H. R. and Varela, F. J. [1992] *The Tree of Knowledge*. Shambhala.

10. Bohm, D. and Peat, F. D. [1989] *Science, Order and Creativity*. Routledge.

11. Capra, F. and Steindl-Rast, D. [1992] *Belonging to the Universe: New Thinking About God and Nature*. Penguin.

12. Sachs, O. [1985] *The Man Who Mistook His Wife For A Hat*. Picador.

13. Capra, F. [1990] *The Turning Point*. Flamingo.

14. Gombrich, E. H. op. cit.

15. Alpers, S. [1983] *The Art of Describing: Dutch Art in the 17th Century*. John Murray.

16. Ibid.

17. Ruskin's view is well described in Walton, P. [1972] *The Drawings of John Ruskin*. Clarendon Press.

Originally published in the *Journal of Art & Design Education*, volume 14 (3) 1995.

Chapter 8: Postmodernism and the Art Curriculum: A New Subjectivity

Malcolm Miles

Introduction

Curricula are designed to transmit bodies of knowledge. But is the idea of a body of knowledge viable? The impact of postmodernism on fields which deal in value and interpretation is unlike that of the identification of previously unrecognized properties of matter on the science curriculum.[1] If generalisations can be made about thought at the end of modernity, one is that the idea of knowledge is negotiable. Postmodern thought sets aside Cartesian certainties and questions what it means to claim to know something, which makes the design of curricula problematic and emphasises investigation of the means of enquiry. There is then a difficulty, characteristic of deconstructive postmodernism, in relating thought to action, for example action to alleviate social injustice.

At this point it is helpful to refer back to the work of the Frankfurt School. Writing in the shadow of the rise of fascism, and despite a disillusionment with liberalism which borders despair, they did not lose hope for a world which was better. It is in this context that they interrogated the relation of the aesthetic and social dimensions of culture, a problem submerged in the self-referential discourses of postmodernism. This paper proposes that the questions raised by the Frankfurt School should form the basis for a review of how and why art is a subject in formal education. This supposes that education has a social purpose, and that art, like critical theory, can be critical of its own production whilst constructing a critique of society. A difficult aspect of its criticality concerns the rationality on which modern society is based, since rationality allows the claim for autonomy, which underpins modernist art and, according to Adorno and Marcuse, constructs its necessary space of critical distance. Another is the question as to whether it is, in Adorno's terms, barbaric to write poetry after Auschwitz.[2] These problems require consideration before attention is given to a curriculum for art, if there is one.

The disenchantment of the world

Rationality stems from fear of reality, substituting for a world of contingencies a self-regulating system of thought. Adorno and Horkheimer state:

> ... *the Enlightenment has always aimed at liberating men [sic] from fear and establishing their sovereignty. Yet the fully enlightened earth radiates disaster triumphant. The programme of the Enlightenment was the disenchantment of the world.*[3]

The kind of knowledge advanced by Enlightenment men such as Bacon is a form of dominance. Freedom from superstition becomes freedom to control. A model in which the shapes of lives are determined from above is replaced by one in which, as it were, the puppets (or some of them) pull the strings. Adorno and Horkheimer list a number of steps along this path: the substitution of animal sacrifice for human sacrifice as an act of representation; the development of representation into universal exchange; then the homogenisation of everything through scientific objectification. They also refer to a 'world of magic (which) retained distinctions whose traces have disappeared even in linguistic form' when multiple affinities are replaced by a single relation of subject and object in which the subject bestows meaning.[4] They do not propose this can be undone, but offer revision within rationality as thought's means of seeing its limitations. Their final sentiment is that 'Enlightenment which is in possession of itself and coming to power can break the bounds of enlightenment.'[5]

Adorno and Horkheimer provide Suzi Gablik, in her book *The Reencbantment of Art*, with a point of departure. She explains:

> *If it is accurate to trace many of our present dilemmas to what has been called the 'disenchantment of the world,' then the solution, presumably, must somehow involve a process that breaks the spell and circle of routines built by modern culture and begins the transition into a different stream of experience.*[6]

Whilst critical theory works through interrogation, Gablik opts for a wholesale rejection of Cartesianism, re-enchanting the disenchanted.

According to Gablik, 'We live in a toxic culture, not just environmentally but spiritually as well.'[7] She argues that social change, in her terms a reversal of ecological damage, requires a new sense of what it means to be alive and conscious in the world: a new subjectivity in place of the Cartesian sense of an isolated self which is the basis of modernity. Rationalism, she argues, devalues imagination and undermines the capacity of art to be compassionate. Gablik refers to contemporary women artists Fern Shaffer and Rachel Dutton who seek to connect with the wisdom traditions of native American peoples, with wilderness experiences and shamanic ritual: 'The shaman can hear the voice of the stones and trees that are speaking.'[8] Which sounds nice for the shaman, and it is easy to dismiss such statements as escapist or demented. But there are a number of issues here, not least the extent to which Gablik's new paradigm is in effect a derivation from what she seeks to overturn, and whether the participatory art she foregrounds is compatible with art's autonomy.

Gablik's case is an extension of currents within modernism. A rejection of the dominant structures of power and value is the basis for the modernist avant-garde.

Equally, pleas for a reclamation of areas of consciousness which industrial capitalism discounts reflect modernism's development out of the Romantic rejection of, and Symbolist withdrawal from, bourgeois society. Matthew Arnold writes of a strange disease of modern life, an iron time of doubts, disputes, distractions and fears. Eliot, in *The Wasteland*, contrasts barges drifting on a river which sweats oil and tar with the gilded barque of Elizabeth and Leicester, and Yeats, whose roots are in pre-Raphaelitism, in *The Lake Isle of Innisfree* conjures a realm of self-sufficiency resembling art for art's sake – Innisfree, too, is a 'value-free' space. Modernism, from its inception, has an ambivalence to the urban-industrial world in which it is produced and consumed. Gablik extends this via a specifically American dream of wilderness, whilst pointing to the (real) toxicity of industrial society.

Perhaps her desire for a new paradigm (though not necessarily its content) is also derived from modernism – modernism as making new. In Descartes' terms, modernity is the drawing of a line according to free imagining. Several writers locate the beginning of modernity in Descartes' *Discourse on the method of rightly conducting reason and seeking for truth in the sciences* [1637]. Claudia Brodsky Lacour writes of 'a common place in histories of Western philosophy and culture that the *Discours de la methode* marks the beginning of modern thought.'[9] Stephen Toulmin states that the 'chief girder in this framework of Modernity ... was the Cartesian dichotomy';[10] and Wolfgang Welsch that 'modern architecture is actually Cartesianism in built form.'[11] Descartes uses the metaphor of architecture for a world of certainty. He states, in a passage of the Discourse which begins with a reminiscence of his sitting in a stove-heated room, that 'buildings which a single architect has undertaken and completed are usually more beautiful and better ordered than those which several architects have attempted to rework'; and contrasts the mess of old cities with 'the well-ordered towns and public squares that an engineer traces on a vacant plain according to his free imaginings.'[12] But if Descartes' model of thought replaces derivation from precedent with making new, it also makes possible, paradoxically, the space of critical reflection and the separation of that space from the world it seeks to change. This problem revolves around the idea of representation.

The power-relation of subject and object reduces the world to categories and concepts. The concept is privileged over the actuality it pre- rather than de-scribes. The separation of aesthetic and scientific knowledges is a form of control through which science becomes 'a system of detached signs devoid of any intention that would transcend the system.'[13] These signs constitute a world reduced to representations which, deprived of immediacy, can be defiled. It is tempting to posit, like Gablik, an art reinvested with value as a way to redress the balance, were it not a fall into the binary pattern which is part of the problem. But it is in any case through the distance between concept and actuality that thought opens a possibility to imagine actuality as other than the way it is. This negation, for Adorno and Marcuse, is the legitimation and limitation of art.

Marcuse states, at the outset of *The Aesthetic Dimension*, that art's autonomy is retained out of despair, but 'expresses a truth, an experience, a necessity' which are 'essential components of revolution.'[14] Art's value is in its space of a subjectivity unmodified by exchange value, in which the dominant order can be ruptured. In his paper to the Dialectics of Liberation Congress in 1967, Marcuse argues that creative imagination will produce radical transformation through a rejection of the performance principle. He foresees 'an "aesthetic" reality – society as a work of art' which is 'the most Utopian, the most radical possibility of liberation today.'[15] This position is echoed in *An Essay on Liberation*, in which he argues that art's power of reconciliation 'adheres even to the most radical manifestations of non-illusory art and anti-art.'[16] But then he alludes to a problem with which Adorno is preoccupied: art draws away from difficult realities such as Auschwitz and My Lai because it cannot represent suffering without aestheticising it; art is 'inexorably infested with this guilt,' though, for Marcuse, it can render such realities impossible again.[17] Adorno is not sure. For him artworks reflect suffering but diminish it by endowing it with acceptability so that 'Art thereby falls into an unsolvable aporia.'[18] When artworks are not consolations in face of a grim reality, they identify with it: 'the most advanced arts push this impoverishment to the brink of silence.'[19] So, in face of Auschwitz, speech which begins to redeem the unspeakable is barbarity.[20] Adorno, always scathing about the culture industries, sees the notion that art can restore 'colour' to the world as something which 'strikes only the artless as possible.'[21] Neither is he very positive about art's social function: 'efforts to restore art by giving it a social function … are doomed.'[22] But for Gablik the spell and circle of modernity can be broken by a renewal of imaginative consciousness, by a new subjectivity: 'at some point, a critical threshold is reached when enough people change their self-images and beliefs to begin the realignment of an entire society.'[23] The means she identifies to achieve this is participatory art for spiritual and ecological healing.

Gablik accepts that some of the art on which she writes is marginal; but it is difficult to relate suggestions of nostalgia for a mythicised wilderness and a misappropriation of other people's cultures when shamanism is mentioned. At the same time, the work of Mierle Ukeles, a sustained campaign to make visible the issue of how waste is handled in New York on which Gablik also writes, does seem to have a capacity to contribute to a change of consciousness amongst the producers of that waste. But as participatory art projects become quietly colonised by the art establishment,[24] there are equally interesting possibilities in art which works within the crevices of modernity, interrogating the basis of knowledge which enables ecological destruction, using its forms to state its futility.

An example is Kate Salway's photographic work *Collectors' Items* [1996]. Groupings of lizards, shells, feathers, insects and butterflies are arranged and photographed in imitation of scientific or collectors' displays. Marbled papers and old engravings lend a nineteenth-century feel to the images. Specimens are set out in a way which isolates each item and permits analysis but ensures the death of the creatures involved. Equal spacing replicates the reduction to homogeneity of the objects of the scientific gaze, and the groupings state a taxonomy oblivious of diversity. All this is a picture of the divisive subjectivity of modernity. But how is this work critical? How does it state negation and avoid the pitfall of aestheticisation of its content (particularly when its subject-matter is composed of natural forms which are a foundation of aesthetic judgment)?

Firstly, the viewer knows these images are photographs, that they are a secondary kind of image, representing a representation. What is useful here is photography's paradoxical inability to re-create reality whilst pretending to offer transparency. But the window through which it leads the spectator is never clear, always coloured by selectivity. Its life is always stilled. Secondly, the arrangement of forms is obviously an artifice. The orderly rows, even their slightly casual misplacing, speak of knowledge as possession, the collector's ownership of specimens as, apart from a psycho-analytical interpretation, 'his' dominance over nature. Thirdly, because the beauty of the images becomes an irony. On closer inspection, these things collected as clues to the life of the skies and oceans reveal their deathliness, their fixedness as signs in a closed system. Elements within the images hint at the above. In some, a black shadow of a window frame falls obliquely on the table on which specimens are spread out, a metaphor for distance. In *Wunderkamme*r, the shadow of the window catch becomes a hook. The shadow, of course, will have moved, if imperceptibly, by the time the photographs are taken.

Salway writes of the cabinets of curiosity first known in Europe in the sixteenth century.[25] Since the management of live exotic animals was difficult, the growing interest in natural history 'was met by the idea of a private collection of curios.'[26] These collections were called *Room of Reason*, *World Theatre* or *Treasure Chamber*, and might be housed in a specially made cabinet – John Evelyn's is exhibited in the Geoffrey Museum in London – or occupy several rooms. These cabinets of curiosity are metaphors for a world which is indisputably known, and, in retrospect, for the subjectivity of modernity. The critical function of Salway's work is in revealing this whilst not replicating it; which is close to Adorno's idea that art works, as Simon Jarvis summarises '... by assembling and organizing materials which ... contain historical experience sedimented within themselves.'[27] By critically reflecting on modernity, Salway's work is as likely to lead to a re-visioning of the world as the participatory art proposed by Gablik.

Praxis

Much remains to work through in Adorno's critique of the aesthetic dimension. If art's unsolvable aporia offers a limit to hope, he would argue it is what is available, that through negation of (and within) what is, unfreedom may be dissolved. What has this to do with the art curriculum? The aesthetic dimension can be mapped onto the University as a space of critical reflection. Like art, academic work neutralises suffering, turns it into text. But, also like art, it is a site for criticality. Its required separateness from everyday life allows the critical distance without which alternative futures could not be imagined. In this respect, art is not different from other discursive disciplines. If it has a curriculum, this is not a matter of the transmission of given taxonomies (of media or of styles) any more than a programme to paint better pictures. It is not, despite the spread of the label as a course title, a matter of art as a social process, but of art as a critical process, of a continuous criticism of society which is inherently political but which can take place as well in the studio as in the street. Adorno and Horkheimer write: 'true revolutionary practice depends on the intransigence of theory in the face of the insensibility with which society allows thought to ossify.'[28] And through praxis – the gaining of understandings of past conditions from which to gain insight into future possibilities – the University contributes to social processes of becoming. Or so it might be. What art in particular has to offer is the imaginative transformation of image and material. Seen as the pursuit of skills (a familiar cry in the period of Thatcherism, and including the skill of self-promotion which characterises some contemporary art) art falls into the dross of the culture industries. Seen as knowledge, but no longer the transmission of a body of knowledge, such transformations are metaphors for radical social change.

Notes and References

1. It can be argued that in some fields, such as mathematics or geometry, a post-modernist reconstruction of what can be called 'known' has little to offer. When a law or theorem has been demonstrated, it remains so forever. This is one reason why Descartes was attracted to these disciplines as offering certainty.

2. Adorno's remark is near the end of an essay on cultural criticism in Prisms, Cambridge [MA], MIT, pp. 19–34.

3. Adorno, T. and Horkheimer, M. [1997] *Dialectic of Enlightenment*, trans. John Cumming. London and New York: Verso.

4. Ibid. p. 10–11.

5. Ibid. p. 208.

6. Gablik, S. [1991] *The Reenchantment of Art*. New York: Thames and Hudson, p. 11.

7. Ibid. p. 24.

8. Ibid. pp. 44–45.

9. Lacour, C. [1996] *Lines of Thought: Discourse, Architectonics, and the Origin of Modern Philosophy*. Duke University Press, p. 18.

10. Toulmin, S. [1990] *Cosmopolis: The Hidden Agenda of Modernity*. University of Chicago Press, p. 108.

11. Welsch, W. [1997] *Undoing Aesthetics*. London and Thousand Oaks, California: Sage, p. 109.

12. Cited in Lacour [1996], p. 33.

13. Adorno and Horkheimer, op. cit., p 18.

14. Marcuse, H. [1978] *The Aesthetic dimension: Toward a Critique of Marxist Aesthetics*. Boston: Beacon, p. 1.

15. Marcuse, H. [1968] *One-Dimensional Man*. Boston, Beacon Press, p. 185.

16. Marcuse, H. [1969] *An Essay on Liberation*. Boston: Beacon, p. 50.

17. Marcuse, 1978, p. 55.

18. Adorno, 1997, p. 39.

19. Ibid. p. 40.

20. Adorno's position could be tested through a critique of the poetry of Paul Celan, a survivor of the Holocaust whose work revolves around this.

21. Ibid. p. 40.

22. Ibid. p. 1.

23. Gablik, op. cit., p. 183.

24. Projects such as 'Conversations at the Castle,' coordinated by Mary Jane Jacob in Atlanta in 1996, show how the organisation of participatory art projects is moving towards more conventional kinds of art curating.

25. For a series of essays on collecting, including curiosities, see Elsner, J. and Cardinal, R. (eds.) [1994] *The Cultures of Collecting*. Reaktion.

26. Salway [1996] p. 48.

27. Jarvis, S. [1998] *Adorno: A Critical Introduction*, New York: Routledge, p. 107.

28. Adorno and Horkheimer, op. cit., p. 41.

Originally published in the *Journal of Art & Design Education*, volume 18 (1) 1999.

Chapter 9: Challenges to Art Education from Visual Culture Studies

Paul Duncum

Overview

Drawing upon recent developments in the movement to reconfigure Art Education as Visual Culture Studies, the author examines three closely related challenges. First, the author considers why art education is being challenged by the field of Visual Culture. Secondly, consideration is given to the challenge to define this emerging field of study in a way that is consistent with the interest art educators have in artefacts that are constitutive of people's values and beliefs. Thirdly, the author critiques how art educators are meeting the challenge to develop pedagogy that is consistent with the nature of visual culture. Finally, a number of further challenges are noted, the most critical being to overcome the gap between theory and policy.

This paper examines three closely related challenges to conventional art education theory and practice now posed by the emergence of Visual Culture Studies.[1] By contrast with conventional art education practice, Visual Culture Studies is primarily concerned with the images of contemporary global media, the ways and conditions under which we look, and a social critique of both. In broad-brush terms, instead of paintings and sculptures, Visual Culture Studies is more concerned with video games, television and theme parks. In equally broad-brush terms, instead of developing the aesthetic gaze, it is more concerned with the numerous ways we look at images, and in place of celebrating art as an expression of human accomplishment, it is interested more in subjecting images to a socio-economic and socio-political analysis.

The paper opens by considering why the emerging field of Visual Culture Studies is challenging art education in the way it is. Secondly, the paper considers how this field of study can be understood in a way that makes sense to art educators. Thirdly, the challenge to develop pedagogy that is consistent with the nature of Visual Culture Studies is examined and some current approaches are critiqued.

Understanding the emergence of Visual Culture Studies

Perhaps this is the least of the challenges, for only the utterly unobservant will have failed to notice what Gitlin calls the torrent of media images that threaten to overwhelm the rest of life in information rich, technologically advanced, globally connected societies.[2] As Stankiewicz[3] says, all advocacy of visual culture, whether as a field of study[4] or as a proposal for a new paradigm within art education,[5] begins by an evocation of the proliferation of imagery within our society. This evocation has been variously conceptualized as a pictorial turn[6] or visual turn[7] a society of spectacle[8] or simply as a society where images are trumping words.[9] Some observers see this development as a good thing,[10] others, as foreshadowing the breakdown of society as we know it.[11]

Whatever perspective is taken, there can be little doubt that an art education that finds its roots in Modernism is challenged by the social conditions and visual technologies of the twenty-first century. They are both fundamentally different from those that pertained during the heyday of Modernism.

If Modernism struggled with ideas of authenticity in an age of reproduced images, today we deal with the proliferation and immediate dissemination of digital images where no original exists and consideration of authenticity makes no sense. Where Modernism was under grid by a more or less clear distinction, at least one that was frequently asserted, between high and low culture, today the two categories are seriously blurred. If it was once possible to assert that culture and commerce were separate, culture and commerce are now equally seen to have imploded so that talk of culture as an industry is now common.[12] Simultaneous with these implosions has been the dramatic escalation of consumerism, a large part of which is packing and promotion but also of cultural products like television programmes, films, videos, and computer games. To continue the expansion of capital, turnover time between production, distribution and consumption must be increasingly shortened, and for this purpose images are a godsend. Image turnover is very much faster than that of white goods, for example. Images proliferate at what seems ever-increasing speed.

In what has become a cornucopia of media images, we are free to participate as we wish, but not free not to participate. Many people find strategies to cope, but whatever approach we adopt we are, according to Gitlin, either churning with the swarming currents of images, trying to keep our heads up, or conscientious objectors trying to clamber to dry land.[13] We variously respond to its temptations by enjoying it, steer through it, or attempt to redirect it, but all the time we try to protect ourselves from it.

Baudrillard argues that increasingly images refer to each other – films to television, television to goods, goods to films, and so on – in an endless cycle hermetically sealed from other kinds of reality.[14] Instead of representing the real, Baudrillard believes that many images are now hyperreal and people can no longer tell what is real. Johnson counters that the problem is not that people confuse the media with the real but that in representing the real in a very limited way, people are prone to limited understandings of what is real.[15]

Either way, the visual culture of corporate capital is everywhere. CNN can now be viewed in some hotel elevators, and even the most private of all spaces, the toilet cubical is no longer sacred. In what are still selected locations, patrons are now forced to watch advertising on small television screens fitted to the back of the cubical door.

If the visual culture of corporate capital is omnipresent, it is equally seductive. Through light and color, movement, shape and texture, through the most exquisite and delicate as well as the most visceral experiences that corporate, global capital can produce. And in an effort to cut through the proliferation of imagery, as well as widespread cynicism about the media, increasingly the appeal of global visual culture is made straight to the nervous system.[16] Bypassing reason, the appeal through sex and violence goes straight to the spinal cord.

In a post traditional society, with traditional sources of identity construction like the church, unions and stable families having eroded, the images of corporate capital also increasingly provide our references for living. We are addressed as consumers, and increasingly people construct themselves as consumers.

A culture of consumerism, however, is in important ways diametrically opposite a prime function of a liberal, general education. Whereas a prime goal of education is to develop a sense of citizenship so that we learn to serve the common good, consumerism puts a premium on individual desire. One is collective: the other, individualistic. Education stresses responsibility and service; consumerism stresses hedonism and pleasure. One stresses going beyond oneself; the other, the accumulation of goods.

Visual Culture Studies has emerged in response to these changed social conditions and technologies. And art educators concerned to meet the challenges of visual culture argue that in the conflict between the citizenship goals of general education and the consumer culture of corporate capital, a reconfigured art education has a significant role to play. Some have accused Visual Culture Studies as being merely a means to educate a more informed consumer,[17] but its goals are for more far-reaching. These goals concern what it means to be both a consumer in a consumer society and a citizen in a democratic society.[18] Not only is citizenship undermined by the logic of capitalism but democracy is at stake when information is limited by the choices offered by a media undergrid by financial interests and not the common good.

The challenge to define visual culture for art education

A second challenge is to define what is to count as visual culture for art education. In attempting to define the more general field of Visual Culture Studies, some advocates cannot even agree on basic terms. Elkins refers to visual culture studies or visual studies,[19] while Mirzoeff argues to retain the term culture to describe the field worrying that the word studies merely implies another academic field while the term culture connotes political struggle over meaning.[20]

In reviewing some notable texts on visual culture, Elkins argues that Visual Culture as a field of study is distinguished less by what it is than what it is not.[21] He claims that it is not especially interested in past cultures, formalism or the canon of western art. Elkins is right on the rejection of formalism and the rejection of a canon, but as a field Visual Culture originated in art history – the term itself originated there[22] – and other texts and anthologies indicate a strong interest in historical imagery.[23] Most texts on visual culture show an interest in the history of both popular and fine art images. Equally, Visual Culture Studies also includes an interest in imagery from science and social science disciplines as diverse as archaeology and zoology and employing as many methodologies. It includes urban planning, interior design, cultural geography, ethnography, military planners, astronomy, anthropology, sociology and so on. It is a conjunction of many issues and interests. In the discussion that follows, I draw upon dominant strands within the field that are primarily concerned with contemporary mass media, what is often called visuality, and a social critique of both. I am especially concerned with the influence of Cultural Studies upon Visual Culture Studies.

Definitions usually come in several forms. First there is a morphological definition where the emphasis is on overthrowing any kind of traditional canon by making as inclusive a list of images as possible. Images may include television programmes, advertising in all its forms, art gallery paintings as well as velvet paintings, art gallery sculpture as well as vernacular lawn sculpture, X-rays, maps, bus timetables, packaging, videos, computer games, lawn furniture, international airports, rock/pop performances, theme parks, graffiti, Barbie, snow globes, book illustrations, fridge magnets, family photographs, and so on and on. This is the most obvious, perhaps because the most visual, of aspects of visual culture; that is, it has a highly promiscuous disposition. What is missed in these lists of miscellaneous images is that they are almost all multimodal in that they contain words and often aural communication as well. Also, what is missed is the rhizomatic[24] and intertextual nature of visual culture where any image relates to other images in a seemingly infinite number of connections through appropriation, parody, irony, and so on.

Secondly, there is a focus on visuality, how we view and use the images of visual culture. The first of these definitions – above – focuses upon the visual in visual culture, the second definition focuses upon the word culture in visual culture. How do we look at artefacts and under what conditions are we allowed or prevented from looking? For example, when do we examine lovingly, with a fleeting glance, with devouring desire, with disinterested detachment (as Kant advised for art), or with a sense of being overwhelmed? When do we look critically like scientists after proof, or like tourists after fleeting sensations, or gaze with religious devotion? When do we glance superficially and when do we scrutinize in depth? Under what conditions do we look? One study Deborah Smith-Shank and I undertook examined self-reports by art educators who as children came across their first 'naughty picture.'[25] We found that for many youngsters 'naughty' was defined as clandestine not by the content of the images – often the pictures were part of scientific discourses – but by the reactions of their peers or parents or the private locations in which the pictures were found.

The third major strand of visual culture – following from the last example – is the focus on context. To the extent to which Visual Culture Studies follows the field of Cultural Studies, this means a number of different contexts. It means the subjective lived experience of audiences as well as the social, economic and political context of images. As a field of study Visual Culture aims to grasp both people's understanding of imagery and the social structures and economic processes and pressures that help determine people's understanding. It concerns itself about people's subjectivity and social structure, lived experience and political struggles.

Visual Culture Studies concerns itself with the intersection of lived experience, power, ideology, and aesthetics. Visual images are seen as tactics in struggles to assert the power of interpretation over issues and groups of people. The old, pre-Hegelian idea of criticism is adopted that to unmask and debunk is a positive contribution to social justice. The ideological nature of the visual culture is of special concern. Visual culture is seen to offer values and beliefs as if they were natural, in the nature of things, as common-sense assumptions about the way things are and beyond which it is impossible to think let alone to contest and offer alternatives. There is nothing so ideological as common sense, nothing that serves the status quo and those who benefit from the status quo, as beliefs and values that are offered as natural. Ideology is masked as common sense, as natural. Ideology works because it is offered in forms that are aesthetically pleasing. Ideas about the world are offered not only as common sense but also in highly seductive ways. For this reason, aesthetics is also very important to many who advocate the study of visual culture.

For the purposes of defining visual culture for art education, it appears fair to say that major trends within Visual Culture Studies are primarily concerned with contemporary and popular imagery, an examination of visuality, and a social critique of both. However, to achieve a critical perspective on contemporary images may often involve cross-cultural and historical studies.

Defining visual culture for art education is a more specific activity. Some art educators have argued against trying to define visual culture, fearing that it is premature to pin down something that is still emerging and fluid. They have particularly objected to the acronym VCAE for Visual Culture Art Education, which has suggested an unfortunate association with the worst of the academic rationalist tendencies of DBAE as funded by the Getty Institute of Education. However, it is seems to me necessary to have some general parameters because, first, if we are unable to offer some kind of clear description of our subject we are left without a hope in the corridors of influence. Additionally, it is not immediately obvious that everything studied as visual culture is a priority for art education or even relevant.

As mentioned above, Visual Culture Studies draws upon many disciplines as well as any number of methodologies, and many do not appear germane to the interests of art educators. I make this assertion in the belief that whatever challenges Visual Culture Studies makes to our theories and practices, one thing remains singularly constant: our interest remains in how people's beliefs and values are communicated through visual imagery. If this is accepted, then many items mentioned in the lists of images above of potential study are not of interest to us, at least not in their intended, original context. Elkins[26] makes a plea not to overlook scientific images and as a field of study he is surely right, but Sturken and Cartwright[27] are closer to our concerns; they examine scientific imagery only insofar as they cross over into a cultural discourse. This principle can be extended to all utilitarian imagery. A road sign for example is of purely utilitarian interest unless it is taken to be more than a sign indicating a particular road and becomes a sign about, for example, what we think about roads or urbanization or modernity, or some other idea bigger then a road itself. Our particular focus as art educators is not purely utilitarian images such as X-rays used to detect bone fractures, or maps that help us find our way around a city, or bus timetables that help us catch transport on time. Only if these items are appropriated to make meaning beyond their originally intended purpose do they become of interest to art educators. Only when they are taken to be cultural signs, posting something about a way, or ways, of life, do they become interesting.

However, this still leaves an enormous number of images of immediate interest and any number of images of potential interest. Since contact time with students is always limited there always exists the need to set priorities so that it is essential to signpost what might be the most fruitful images to examine in the classroom. Bolin and Blandy have argued for the widest possible range of artefacts under the rubric of material culture.[28] They would include everything from the common pin to interplanetary space vehicles, meat cuts, plowed fields, and even the gaseous shapes we form when speaking are potentially of interest to them. They write, '… nothing affected by human agency is overlooked as too insignificant for intensive examination, nor viewed as too small for eliciting substantive meaning.'[29] They show that seemingly trivial items can have deep personal significance to their owners, evoking long-forgotten but keen memories.

In their favour, it is a fact that the least image can be made meaningful by creative imagination. However, since priorities must be set, I would argue for beginning with the more obvious forms of communication, those that affect all students on a daily basis and increasingly form their reference points for living. Meat cuts, plowed fields and gaseous shapes are not obvious candidates. The obvious candidates are the principle cultural forms of corporate, global capital, namely television – which is often called the national curriculum – computer games, movies and videos, advertising, and so on. These cultural forms do not need to be appropriated to make meaning; they come embodied with other people's meaning and about which we must make decisions whenever we are exposed to them. Considering that we are exposed to about 3000 commercial impressions a day,[30] this means making decisions all day, every day. Whether we warm to it or not, our priorities as art educators are set by the participation of our students in the commercial corporate culture in which they, and we, live. This does not mean, of course, that the way we study cultural forms is set by commercial interests, a point that leads to consider the development of pedagogy that meets the challenge of visual culture.

The challenge to develop appropriate pedagogy

As I write late in 2004, art educators appear to be practicing at least six relatively distinct pedagogies all under the rubric of visual culture, though some appear more valid than others. My comments are taken from the literature, conference presentations, discussions with colleagues, and classroom observations.

First, students are being asked to respond in their own idiosyncratic ways to popular culture in a conventional art form such as painting, collage, or ceramics. This approach is modelled after conventional best art education practice where student work arises from their own understandings and preoccupations. The approach is sometimes promoted as ideas development. However, there is a serious disconnect with this approach, where critiquing twenty-first-century cultural forms is followed by a response in pre-industrial revolution cultural forms.

Thinking in the media has long been one of the justifications for visual arts education, although in the past twenty or so years art education has been effectively constituted by two strands, creativity and critique, or making and appraisal. These strands are conceptualized as interconnected, the one supporting the other. Making is seen to provide an insider's perspective on how artists make images, which informs student appraisal of artists' work, while appraisal is seen to provide students with a wealth of material to draw upon in creating their own work. This has worked well with traditional media, but a disconnect emerges when students are asked to critique a sitcom, for example, but then they are asked to respond by making silkscreen prints.

Third, students are being asked to follow the work of contemporary artists who respond in their work to popular visual culture.[31] The key word in the last sentence is follow. Students are typically asked to examine the work of an artist and then create something like the work of the artist. This approach sometimes involves following an artist's ideas such as Cindy Sherman with Barbie dolls or the form of an artist's work such as with Barbara Kruger. The advantage of this approach is that it comes armed with a critical edge as well as relying upon the parent practice of art. However, as Hermann argues, there is also a serious disconnect with this approach where students are not asked to research and process issues the way artists have, but to follow the already expressed ideas of artists.[32] With this approach, the subject matter has changed, but the lock-step, follow-the-leader process remains the same as much of DBAE practice.

Fourth, students are being asked to create parallel forms of contemporary media, usually magazines,[33] newspapers or videos. These forms usually turn out to be parodies, relying upon student's intuitive knowledge of these forms and adolescent love of having fun with adult culture. The approach is well tested from media education,[34] and the new digital technologies such as Photoshop and iMovie programmes make these parallel forms increasingly look professional. The advantage of this approach is that students can make images using virtually – sometimes identical – technologies as they critique, and so think in the media they critique.

Fifth, there are numerous practices developed under the rubric of material culture with the intention of telling personal, often deeply moving stories about the connections between people and objects.[35] The approach tends to privilege subjectivity over social structure, a celebration of individual narrative over a consideration of social critique. While validly derived from Material Culture Studies, it does not reflect the socially critical edge of Visual Culture Studies. It tends not to ask the kind of questions explored below about social structure, economics and political struggle.

Sixth, a growing number of art educators are adopting versions of a practice originally developed by Marjorie Wilson to deal with DBAE[36] but now often using popular visual culture as a starting point. This is a research-cum-expressive project that starts with a single image but broadens out to include other texts such as other images, poems, song lyrics, film clips, and so on, all produced through hyperlinking computer programmes, and often built up from material retrieved from the Web. Some of these exercises use StorySpace or Dreamweaver, but remarkable results are possible even with an imaginative use of PowerPoint. This approach can be also undertaken with paste and paper, but the use of computer programmes makes the retrieval and juxtaposition of images and other text very much faster. With StorySpace, viewers can also rearrange connections between images and other texts to their own liking and so create new connections. The approach has the virtue of emphasizing the rhizomatic, intertextual and multimodal nature of visual culture.

Students begin with an image to which they are personally drawn. For example, one of Tavin's students worked on an advertisement for Levi's jeans that he linked to many other images and written texts that similarly constructed race as non-threatening.[37] Another student investigated a Nike advertisement, exploring images that embodied ideas as diverse as patriarchy, globalization and commoditization. My own graduate and undergraduate students have worked on such diverse images as advertisements for fashion clothes, ice cream and gymnasiums; photojournalism; PEZ dispensers; sitcoms; TV reality programmes; TV dating programmes; ice hockey; violent video games; and Las Vegas casinos. For example, one student began with a high-gloss magazine advertisement by fashion designer Versace. The picture showed thin, blonde models in a plush, faux baroque dinning room wearing elegant gowns. The student used the picture as a springboard to explore both health issues and wealth, two constructions that were evident from the picture. She included numerous pictorial, statistical and literary texts that showed and commented upon both anorexia and the massive asymmetry of wealth and poverty in the US.

Layered over some of the above approaches, students are required to ask a range of questions, including questions drawn from aesthetics, semiotics, ethnography, sociology and cultural theory. Among aesthetic questions, students are encouraged to ask, for example: what do I experience when watching a particular television programme? Am I excited, bored, thrilled, alternatively bored and thrilled, and so on? Which parts are exciting and which are something else? Why are certain parts far more interesting than others? What do I find attractive? Is it the characters, my knowledge of the actors, the way they are in conflict, the camera movements, the lighting, and so on? These questions help tease out what draws an audience in, and they are essential in understanding much of the appeal of a cultural site.

Commonly, students undertake semiotic analysis. For example, they ask of particular cultural sites: Are they racist? or sexist? or xenophobic? or homophobic? Do they privilege some people over others? Do they marginalize some people or some issues? What techniques are used to marginalize people or issues? Do they offer stereotypes of some groups of people? Students ask: Are the values embodied by a television programme contradictory? For example, do some programmes condemn violence as a way of conflict resolution only to include a great deal of violence? And looking beyond isolated programmes, students ask: Are the values of one programme contradicted by another?

Recognizing that it is never good enough to assume that we know from the images themselves what other people think, students are also asked to undertake ethnographic work. They ask about how images are interpreted by others. How are images understood in terms of people's lived experience, in terms of what people make of the images and just how they weave them into their lives? Students do their own market research, asking their friends and relatives and their own students, of course, as well as gleaning what they can from published research. I encourage students not to assume that people simply adopt the position of the image-makers. Students ask: Do people resist the intended meaning of a cultural site? Do people negotiate meaning, accepting some aspects but reject or remain doubtful about other aspects? Do they even understand the intended meaning? This kind of ethnographic work may simply involve students undertaking surveys of opinion or knowledge; students ask other students or parents for their opinions, or they visit shops and ask proprietors and customers. For example, I have witnessed third-graders ask visiting souvenir shops and quizzing tourists about their purchases.[38]

Extending out to the social structure itself, students also ask questions about the institutions that produce images. Who owns particular cultural sites and what else do they own? The answer to this question will not only help explain all the cross promotion and product placements within cultural sites but help explain what is rarely if ever mentioned. Asking what is not on television, or discussed in other forms of popular culture, can be highly instructive. Students ask: What are the primary functions of cultural sites? What values and beliefs do they embody and impart? For example, it surprises some of my adult students to learn that commercial television does not exist to show programmes, but to show advertisements, and that from an economic point of view, from the perspective of the advertisers and the owners of television stations, it is the programmes that are the breaks between advertisements. From a socioeconomic perspective, television exists to sell things, but not just things. Television also sells an ideology of consumerism; in selling the benefits of consuming more and more things it sells consumerism as a way of life, as a culture of consumerism. It constructs viewers as consumers, and consumerism is presented – to refer to something I wrote earlier – as natural, as in the way of things. Today, media companies are vertically integrated, and perhaps they are better known as media conglomerates. They own television stations, film studios, football teams, record labels, clothing brands, and so on, and each medium is used to sell other media owned by the same company. It is useful to ask how much money is involved in any one cultural site. It helps to get an idea of our priorities as a society. This can be challenging work for students, though often a single critical question will set off the kind of cognitive dissonance that leads to adopting a more general critical perspective.

Further challenges

In introducing visual culture to art education there are other challenges. One challenge is to assist colleagues who have little understanding of visual culture as a field but who nevertheless call their practice visual culture. It is possible to be scuttled more by those who have picked up visual culture as the latest fad than by serious-minded opponents. Another challenge is to deal with opponents, with the backlash now erupting from art educators steeped in modernism and for whom visual culture appears to threaten their most cherished ideals.[39] Ralph Smith, for example, warns of dire consequences for art education if Visual Culture Studies is allowed to take over.[40] A more substantial problem, however, the biggest now faced by proponents of visual culture in art education, is how the modernist versus postmodernist divide works itself out in relation to policy and assessment. There exists a huge gap between the ideas explored in this paper and the standardized testing that is now encroaching upon schools at seemingly every level.

Stankiewicz rightly points to a gap between theory and policy.[41] The kind of postmodern theories that inform advocacy for visual culture studies emphasize diversity, fragmentation, and individual exploration, while government instrumentalists increasingly stress standards established through multichoice knowledge tests. One is under grid by the postmodern assumptions; the other, by the worst of Modernist rationalizing tendencies towards social engineering. Stankiewicz is correct in warning that, while Visual Culture Study has much to recommend it, unless this divide is bridged, Visual Culture Studies will not significantly impact Art Education as a whole. It will remain only a worthy proposal for a new paradigm, not a paradigm itself. This challenge needs to be met at a systems level, but it also needs to be met from the classroom up. We need material on exemplary classroom practices to meet the resistance to change among teachers that always stymie the best-developed theory. At least towards this challenge, a number of publications are currently underway.[42]

Notes and References

1. This paper follows a similar structure to one published early in 2002 in the *International Journal of Art and Design Education* but it is completely rewritten to take advantage of debates and developments that have emerged since then.

2. Gitlin, T. [2001] *Media Unlimited: How the Torrent of Images and Sounds Overwhelms Our Lives.* New York: Metropolitan Books.

3. Stankiewicz, M. A. [2004] 'A Dangerous Business: Visual Culture Theory and Education Policy,' *Arts Education Policy Review*, 105, no. 6, pp. 5–13.

4. For example, Barnard, M. [1998] *Art, Design and Visual Culture*, London: Macmillan; Elkins, J. [2003] *Visual Studies: A Skeptical Introduction*, New York: Routledge; Mirzeoff, N. [2001] *An Introduction to Visual Culture,* London: Routledge; Sturken, M. and Cartwright, L. [2001] *Practices of Looking: An Introduction to Visual Culture*, Oxford: Oxford University Press; and Walker, J. and Chaplin, S. [1997] *Visual Culture: An Introduction*, Manchester: Manchester University Press.

5. For example, Duncum, P. [2002] 'Theorising Everyday Aesthetic Experience with Contemporary Visual Culture,' *Visual Arts Research*, 28, no. 2, pp. 4–15; Freedman, K. [2003] *Teaching Visual*

Culture: Curriculum, Aesthetics, and the Social life of Art, New York: Teachers College Press; and Tavin, K. [2003] 'Wrestling with Angels, Searching for Ghosts: Towards a Critical Pedagogy of Visual Culture,' *Studies in Art Education*, 44, no. 3, pp. 197–213.

6. Mitchell, W. J. T. [1994] *Picture Theory: Essays on Verbal and Visual Representation*. Chicago: Chicago University Press.

7. Jenks, C. (ed.) [1995] *Visual Culture*. London: Routledge.

8. Debord, G. [1967/1977] *Society of the Spectacle*. Detroit, MI: Black & Red.

9. Guinness, O. [1994] *Fit Bodies, Fat Minds: Why Evangelicals Don't Think and What To Do About It*. Grand Rapids, MC: Hourglass Books.

10. For example, Johnson, S. [1997] *Interface Culture: How New Technology Transforms the Way We Create and Communicate*, San Francisco, CA: HarperEdge.

11. For example, Baudrillard, J. [1987] *The Evil Demon of Images*, Sydney: Power Institute of Fine Arts; Jameson, F. [1998] *The Cultural Turn: Selected Writings on the Postmodern, 1983–1998*, London: Verso, and Guinness, *Fit Bodies, Fat Minds*.

12. Williams, R. [1983] *Keywords: A Vocabulary of Culture and Society*, 2nd ed. London: Fontana.

13. Gitlin, op. cit.

14. Baudrillard, op. cit.

15. Johnson, op. cit.

16. Jhally, S. (Producer/Writer/Director) [1996] *Advertising and the End of the World*. [Motion picture]. Available from Media Education Foundation, 60 Masonic Street, Northampton, MA 01060.

17. Krauss, R. [1996] *Welcome to the Cultural Revolution*. October. 77, pp. 83–96.

18. Freedman, op. cit.

19. Elkins, op. cit.

20. Mirzeoff, op. cit.

21. Elkins, op. cit.

22. See Baxandall, M. [1972] *Paintings and Experience in Fifteenth-Century Italy: A Primary in the History of Pictorial Style*. Oxford: Clarendon Press.

23. For example, Bryson, N., Holly, M. and Moxey, K. [1994] *Visual Culture: Images and Interpretations*, Hanover, NH: University Press of New England; and Jenks, *Visual Culture*.

24. Think of grass; it spreads laterally and as soon as one part is damaged it grows elsewhere. The internet is another rhizomatic structure. Rhizomes have no core; they are made up of an infinite number of chains.

25. Duncum, P. and Smith-Shank, D. L. [2001] 'Naughty Pictures: Their Significance in Initial Sexual Identity Formation,' *Journal of Social Theory in Art Education*, 21, pp. 91–113.

26. Elkins, op. cit.

27. Sturken and Cartwright, op. cit., chapter 8.

28. Bolin, P. E. and Blandy, D. [2003] 'Beyond Visual Culture: Seven Statements of Support for Material Culture in Art Education, *Studies in Art Education*, 44, no. 3, pp. 246–263.

29. Ibid., p. 250. It is noteworthy that despite their inclusiveness, when they come to justify the study of material culture in terms of social significance their examples – the anti-social nature of excessively violent video games – are precisely those that champions of visual culture have used.

30. Jhally, op. cit.

31. See examples in Gaudelius, Y. and Speirs, P. (eds.) [2002] *Contemporary Issues in Art Education*. Upper Saddle River, NJ: Prentice Hall.

32. Herrmann, R. [2004] *Making Art Education Relevant to Students and Consistent with Contemporary Art Practice*. Masters Thesis, University of Illinois at Urbana Champaign.

33. Blandy, D. and Congdon, K.G. [2003] 'Using Zines ot Teach About Postmodernism and the Communication of Ideas,' *Art Education*, 56, no. 3, pp. 44–52.

34. See, for example, Buckingham, D. and Sefton-Green, J. [1994] *Cultural Studies Goes to School: Reading and Teaching Popular Media*. London: Taylor & Francis.

35. Bolin, P. [2004] *People, Stories and Objects*, paper presented at the National Art Education Association Conference, Denver, April.

36. Wilson, M. [2001] 'The Text, the Intertext, and the Hypertextual: A Story,' *2000 International Visual Arts Conference: Art Education and Visual Culture*, Taipei: Taipei Municipal Teachers College, pp. 89–107.

37. Tavin, K. [2002] 'Engaging Advertisements: Looking for Meaning In and Through Art Education,' *Visual Arts Research*, 28, no. 2, pp. 38–47.

38. Duncum, P. [2001] 'Theoretical Foundations for an Art Education of Global Culture and Principles for Classroom Practice,' *International Journal of Education & the Arts*, 2, no. 3. An electronic journal at http://ijea.asu.edu/v2n3/

39. For example, Eisner, E. 'Should we create new aims for art education?' *Art Education*, 54, no. 5, pp. 6–10; Peter J. Smith, 'Visual culture studies verses art education,' *Arts Education Policy Review*, 104, no. 4, 3–9.

40. Smith, R. [2004] 'Introduction: Visual Culture Studies. Part Two,' *Arts Education Policy Review*, 106, no. 1, pp. 3–4.

41. Stankiewicz, op. cit.

42. For example, Duncum, P. (ed.) *Visual Culture in the Art Class: Case Studies* (Reston: VA: National Art Education Association) is due for publication release in 2006.

Originally published in the *Journal of Art & Design Education*, volume 21 (1) 2002.

Chapter 10: Who's Afraid of Signs and Significations? Defending Semiotics in the Secondary Art and Design Curriculum

Nicholas Addison

Semiotics remains something of a dirty word for art and design teachers in schools. It is often perceived as a hopelessly indulgent method employed by male academics bent on constructing over-complicated systems of analysis in pursuit of an object of study that few of them can agree upon. It has been suggested that the import of all this activity could be more simply stated by people who do not have methodological axes to grind, those not frightened by a bit of common sense.[1] But this is to miss the point. The common belief that art reflects or mirrors reality encourages people to overlook the ways that representational practices are used to construct the symbolic formations that come to be understood as truths. Semiotics enables people to ask awkward questions to challenge the naturalised status of these cultural forms and practices, especially the network of normative values that are reproduced through the process of schooling. From the position of traditional art education, therefore, semiotics is undoubtedly an alien and corrupting influence, a method contaminated by its association with both linguistic semiology and that great 'other' cultural studies; art in schools is fearful of methodological contamination.[2] Alternatively, from the positions of postmodern education, positions that acknowledge the inclusive agendas of, say, postfeminism and postcolonialism, semiotics is already moribund, tainted by its collusion with modernist metanarrative and imperial in its ambition. Additionally, the hybrid and formless nature of postmodernism's anointed vehicle, multi-media, is seen as foreign to semiotics which appears bound to structuralist principles and is therefore constipated in an age of fluidity. In schools, for whatever the reason and from whichever perspective, the potential accessibility of semiotic methods for both the reception and production of art is avoided.

Kerry Freedman states one such critical position:

> *The meaning of technological images cannot be simply understood in terms of what has been called 'visual literacy,' which has generally meant the semiotic reading of signs and symbols …… the concept of visual literacy is an attempt to force images to fit illegitimately into a structuralist analysis of literary texts that tends to narrow visual meaning. Rather a broad view of creative production and interpretation in relation to multiple meanings and visual qualities is called for if we are to understand and teach about the use of images in contemporary life.[3]*

These sentiments are the product of misapprehensions. Semiotics is not synonymous with linguistics and/or literary criticism rather it belongs to a tradition which seeks to define systems of communication other than language.[4] This is an important quest in order to understand the multimodal nature of learning in secondary schools especially when language, particularly writing, holds a privileged position there. Art (and design) is positioned as 'other' within this logocentric curriculum and there is a danger for art and design teachers to separate out and valorise the visual as somehow ineffable, above and beyond the grasp of reasoned analysis. For semioticians, the disciplinary divisions that separate out expressive and communicative acts are not substantive, analytical categories as they are say for aestheticians, rather they are cultural practices indicative of the hierarchical distinctions used to perpetuate forms of legitimacy. Therefore semioticians have no need to differentiate between or within types of art object unlike traditional art critics and historians who are bound to a series of self-perpetuating oppositions: fine/applied, genius/artisan, primitive/decadent. Instead semioticians increasingly interrogate the matrix of meaning that results from the interrelationship between modes of production and reception, an interrogation that is social in orientation.

The accusation that semiotics has remained inert and stuck in a rigid structuralist paradigm is equally suspect; poststructuralist semiotics admits no closure:

> *Derrida, in particular, insisted that the meaning of any particular sign could not be located in a signified fixed by the internal operations of a synchronic system; rather, meaning arose exactly from the movement from one sign or signifier to the next, in a* perpetuam mobile *where there could be found neither a starting point for semiosis, nor a concluding moment in which semiosis terminated and the meanings of signs fully 'arrived.'[5]*

However, such openness, uncertainty and ambivalence are situated uncomfortably within a curriculum that demands measurable outcomes and clearly defined bodies of knowledge. Therefore, when considering the possibility of a postmodern curriculum it is essential to examine the institutional host (the school) by which it is to be framed. Universal secondary education is a modernist phenomenon.[6] The inclusion of art and design in the curriculum is equally a product of modernist utopian philosophies, whether utilitarian, conceiving design education as answering to the needs of industry and thus the common good, or aesthetic, responding to innate critical and creative faculties to enable personal actualisation. Neither of these seems to hold much cogency or viability for schools any longer so art and design is in a crisis of identity. Squeezed by rationalisation, threatened by technology and media studies it takes up defensive positions. A radical and wholesale shift to postmodern strategies appears to be a proactive answer; but art and design cannot take on the position of postmodern vanguard alone. Nevertheless, within the modernist structures of education the case for postmodern intervention as a form of resistance is well made,[7] a process that echoes the built-in critique of modernism practised by the avant-garde within the history of twentieth-century art. Hal Foster elucidates the potential for continuous critical self-renewal:

> *Thus was formal modernism plotted along a temporal, diachronic, or vertical axis: in this respect it opposed an avant-gardist modernism that did intend 'a break with the past'- that, concerned to extend the area of artistic competence, favoured a spatial, synchronic, or horizontal axis. A chief merit of the neo-avant-garde … is that it sought to keep these two axes in critical coordination …it worked through its ambitious antecedents, and so sustained the vertical axis or historical dimension of art. At the same time it turned to past paradigms to open up present possibilities, and so developed the horizontal axis or social dimension of art as well.[8]*

By neglecting semiotics art and design teachers are avoiding their 'ambitious antecedents' and failing to adopt methods that would enable them to question art practices so as to break the insularity of much current classroom practice. Furthermore, semiotics is close to pupils' own modes of meaning-making in ways that logic, mathematics, formalist aesthetics and other systems that share a privileged status in the school curriculum are not:

> *Compared with logic it (semiotics) is highly pragmatic, because the inferences with which it is concerned are ones which pervade our everyday lives. They are the inferences by which we make sense, or fail to make sense, of our environment. Semiotics is profoundly social, because of the fundamental role which signs play in every moment of human life and of our interaction in society.[9]*

Classroom practice

Although there is still much potential for its neglect, the National Curriculum has ensured that the critical reception of art cannot be disregarded. Despite Thistlewood's heresies[10] and an increasing literature, critical and contextual studies is at best a secondary observance servicing the primary concern of making, its significance in the classroom is far from secure.[11] What then is happening at the point of delivery?

Research highlights the modernist canon that lies at the centre of primary and secondary education up to and including GCSE.[12] Pupils learn to transcribe and pastiche exemplary sources and occasionally integrate some technical or stylistic feature, pointillism, fragmentation, and apply it to their own observations. One might argue that the Eurocentric historical period chosen (approximately thirty years either side of 1900) is appropriate to the focus of GCSE which emphasises personal response accommodated within the orthodoxy of working from observation. With young children transcription is a revealing process because they select from the image to be 'copied' those things or features which hold most interest for them. At secondary level, with its analytical imperatives and tools, the process of transcription focuses on the more superficial task of the imitation of surface. This is not without its benefits, but it is a time-consuming task that offers no understanding of either the process of making (the pupil imitates the outcome, usually a photographic reproduction, not the practice of transforming perceptions/conceptions into sensible form) nor any historical or contextual investigation. Thus, at GCSE, 'A' Level and AVCE, the critical and contextual sketch-book is all too often a collection of transcriptions (some annotated), drawings and pamphlets from exhibitions, written personal responses to favoured images, extracts copied from art historical texts and serendipitous reproductions. It often possesses great energy and enthusiasm, seems to indicate visual investigation, but in truth has only its 'look,' closer inspection reveals appropriation, imitation, material exploration and variation.

Dyson, Taylor, Parsons, Csikszentmihalyi, Schofield, Cunliffe, Dawtrey et al. and Addison[13] have suggested useful methods by which art and design can be critically approached in the classroom. Most will no doubt be criticised for belonging to modernist paradigms, whether those of developmental psychology, structuralism, humanist universalism, disinterested aestheticism or cultural studies. Some teachers possessing an art historical background may in addition use formalist and/or iconographic methods, for example, respectively, those of Wolfflin (1915)[14] and Panofsky (1955) who are both part of a modernist critical tradition. As such, their methods depend on analytical processes that are sequential and developmental and may, therefore, seem inappropriate, especially at Key Stage 3, because there is little time to incorporate their use in any sustained and rigorous way. It is unlikely, therefore, that pupils would be able to assimilate and apply these methods independently or in other analytical contexts. What interpretive methods do pupils tend to use in their everyday lives? I would argue that they use semiotics, they seek clues as to a person's personality, status, and accessibility through categories of signs. They interpret external signs such as clothes, body forms, posture, simultaneously with interactive ones such as gestures, speech, responsive actions and so on. This is the process of interpretation that should be built upon in the classroom. On one level the way in which such processes can be applied to representational art is obvious, represented indicators like gesture being decoded in the same way. But this transference from life to art would suggest that the vehicle of representation, its material base and formal organisation, is neutral as if it were independent of meaning: the old form/content dichotomy.

Inclusion and postmodernity

The contemporary field of images is extraordinarily diverse and inclusive, historical and multicultural ones no more or less than others, and the national curriculum requires that this diversity be addressed. How, therefore, can teachers enable pupils to understand art objects from cultural and historical sources that use signifying systems different to their own? After all these objects, familiarised through reproductions, are often known in appropriated, decontextualised or recontextualised forms. For example, for Roman Catholics the infant Christ held in the lap of the Virgin, the Madonna and Child, is a sign that conventionally represents the incarnation, the signified (concept) 'god made flesh,' or more specifically, with the compositional focus on the child's penis, 'god made man.'[16] However, in conjunction with the humanity of Mary, the mother and child union is also a sign that embodies a related signified, the purity and divinity of motherhood. When this is represented by Masaccio (1401–28) in *The Virgin and Child* (1426) in contrast to *The Virgin and Child before a Firescreen* (1440) by a follower of Campin (active 1406–44) (both in the National Gallery, London), the technical and representational resources, the 'signifiers,' produce contrasting effects. On the one hand, in the Masaccio, both the mis-en-scène and the technical manner are hieratic and austere while in contrast Mary's expression is tender. On the other hand, in the Flemish work, the surroundings are domestic, the manner naturalistic and detailed and Mary's actions somewhat brusque; thus for audiences the signification in each case is inflected by representational resources that indicate the ideological differences of the maker's habitus and the interpretative communities for which the paintings were produced. My descriptions are themselves formed in relation to my particular subject position, and I make sense of them because of my particular interests and the relationship between my ideological position and those embodied in the paintings. My position is produced within specific secular and materialist discourses and it is therefore unlikely to correspond neatly with interpretations by Protestant, or Catholic, or Muslim communities.

Similarly, Cornelia Parker's piece *Cold Dark Matter* from 1991 has been interpreted by some as an attack on the father and patriarchy. This interpretation was elicited by reading the object of the explosion, a garden shed (typically a private domestic space for men) as a symbol for the father's psyche (the shed being both a repository and a potential), and by reading the British army (the organisation commissioned to carry out the explosion) as an institutional index of homosocial, hierarchised, British patriarchy. The explosion thus plays on the private/public dichotomy of masculine power whereby male aggression, at the behest of a 'femme fatale,' destroys its most private domain and in the process exposes the secrets of the masculine desire, a political act. Parker, in conversation with the feminist art historian Lisa Tickner[17] discusses a range of interpretative responses to the work and Tickner notes the gendered identity of the shed. Parker responds: 'That's the kind of interpretation I'm always trying to avoid: the shed is the male domain and therefore … I don't talk about personal issues or psychology. It's always about maintaining a space for the work.'[18] However, a little later she generously states:

And then I think being an artist is such a political thing in its own right. Just the fact that you're doing what you're doing is a political act, but I'm always trying to maintain a certain openness to interpretation. I want the work to tell me things, to surprise me, so that the work is kind of waste product from a process, an inquiry you started when you didn't know the answers at all. Later, in retrospect, you can talk eloquently about it but when you're in the middle of it you can't.[19]

As the meaning of the work of art is made anew in each interpretative act, what meanings come to hold validity at a particular moment of time depend on the power relations within interpretative communities, and at present the validity of different subject positions is increasingly recognised by art historians who acknowledge the lead provided by semiotics:

Once launched into the world, the work of art is subject to all of the vicissitudes of reception; as a work involving the sign, it encounters from the beginning the ineradicable fact of semiotic play. The idea of convergence, of causal chains moving toward the work of art should, in the perspective of semiotics, be supplemented by another shape: that of lines of signification opening out from the work of art, in the permanent diffraction of reception.[20]

In secondary schools the art and design teacher therefore has the difficult task of both substantiating privileged knowledge while simultaneously recognising the validity of different (relative?) positions. Should they revive the critical methods and criteria from the maker's culture or period, or should they have recourse to familiar and current methods? If teachers encourage the clue seeking most usually employed by pupils, they would need to complement it by providing, or asking pupils to research, contextual information. Without it pupils would be unable to decode what are likely to be relatively opaque sign systems. However, teachers should be careful not to impose preconceived structures in such a way as to predetermine interpretation. Thomas Puttfarken[21] demonstrates how, in bypassing traditional methods in favour of semiotic 'detective' work, one can strip away years of formalist misinterpretation. In his analysis of Caravaggio's paintings on the 'Story of St Matthew,' he attends to the sort of details which can be marginalised in formalist accounts. This allows him to question received notions about the determining role of such privileged signifiers as compositional rhetoric and leads him to a radical reinterpretation:

We know that in good detective stories the person caught with a smoking gun or a blood stained knife is not the murderer. To traditional admirers of Caravaggio's art, in fact of most European art, this may seem an entirely inappropriate attitude to adopt in front of his masterpieces. Yet I believe it is an attitude which we are invited to adopt by the picture itself (The Martyrdom of St Matthew) … we find that the close scrutiny of details belies the obvious display of pictorial composition. Expecting to witness the

*murder of the saint, we have virtually no option but to see the nude man with the
sword as attacking Matthew; this is the logic of pictorial normality, and the immediate
visual evidence seems fully to confirm our expectations. Yet in carefully observing and
considering the details of dress, movement and expression, we come to a different
conclusion.*[22]

The 'what' and the 'how'

The ways in which semiotics as an academic discipline can add to the everyday
process is in its concern not only with the 'what' of signs, but in the 'how.' When
considering how signs work in art it is necessary to examine them as signifying
through a series of relationships. Thus the artwork is not a repository of meaning
but a site for meaning-making. Seen from this perspective its multiple signifiers;
materials, composition, modality, in combination with its signifieds;
representations, ideology, allusions, become an interrelated system through which
meaning is actively produced. These meanings are not fixed in any intentionalist or
affective way but are constructed through an interactive relationship between a
work (no doubt once replete with intentions) and a perceiver and are thus open to
difference and multiple significations. How the signifier relates to its signified
(form with concept) and how in turn the perceiver relates the resulting sign to a
referent (an experience or thing in the world) is the interesting question. How does
the sender relate to the receiver? How is meaning altered by investigating the
contexts of the artwork's making? Which contexts are significant? Who produces
the meaning? How are intentions and interpretations negotiated? Where is
meaning situated? In the artwork, in one or more of the active participants or
somewhere outside and between them? By understanding how a system of signs
works pupils are enabled to consider not just the content or technique of their own
work and its relationship to exemplars, but their own practice, looking and making,
as a method for the production of meaning and as a vehicle for communication.

Some commentators have argued that art historical methods are semiotic,[23] if so,
why introduce a new terminology for something that already exists? Formalism,
iconography and even connoisseurship, in their separate ways, isolate the work of
art from its subjective and social dimensions. They posit objective systems that can
produce 'right' or 'appropriate' attributions and interpretations through the
retrieval of intentions (on the intentional fallacy see Preziosi.[24]) The new semiotics
is more concerned with the uses of art, understanding the social application and
transformation of artefactual codes, than in reinforcing the status of art as
autonomous and ineffable. Nonetheless formalist methods might be seen as a
proto-semiotic in that they answer:

*... the perfectly legitimate concern to assert the specificity of artistic, and principally
plastic phenomena, and to preserve their study from any contamination by verbal
models, whether linguistic or psychoanalytic, since the characteristic articulation and*

At the beginning of the twentieth century the desire to map out the semic territory of a particular expressive and communicative mode, here the plastic arts, must have seemed urgent, a task giving credence to the hard-won position of (illusory?) autonomy which unburdened artists, however briefly, of their previous function as recorders and propagandists to power, servants to texts and design. Wolfflin's system of formalist, binary oppositions has particular similarities to the self-consciously semiotic system formulated later by the anthropologist Levi-Strauss,[26] itself Saussurean in derivation. Although Wolfflin's method, like any other, can be applied as a blunt or subtle instrument, its basic tenet, the interrogation of an artwork through the imposition of associated oppositions, has very real possibilities for use with school pupils: in his case; linear/painterly, plane/recession, closed/open form, multiplicity/unity, absolute/relative clarity,[27] in Levi-Strauss' profane/sacred, cooked/raw, celibacy/marriage, female/male, central/peripheral. Wolfflin's formal and Levi-Strauss' social oppositions might be usefully extended through issue-based oppositions, e.g. conservation/redevelopment, purity/hybridity, popular/elite, genetic/social.

Iconographic analysis, or even its Panofskian extension into iconology, contains the danger of assuming that the vehicle, or in semiotic terms the signifier, is neutral (an issue identified above). Here the artwork's content (the signified) is delivered by its material means (signifiers) in a seamless process of transmission where only the symbolic nature of its represented objects stands in the way of literal interpretation. The iconographer's job is then to decode the represented symbols: to do this they need recourse to originating texts (in the beginning was the word):

It means introducing into the analysis of the picture the authority of the text from which the picture is supposed to derive its arrangement through a kind of figurative and/or symbolic application, in which each pictorial element corresponds to a linguistic term ... iconography as a method, is theoretically founded on the postulate that the artistic image (indeed any relevant image) achieves a signifying articulation only within and because of the textual reference which passes through and eventually imprints itself in it.[28]

The insertion of art historical methods to support and provide academic credibility to a 'recreational' or 'vocational' subject might appear to be a tempting strategy. But the insularity of iconographic and/or formalist analysis is likely to prove an alienating experience for pupils hoping to learn about the relationship between the diversity of visual cultures and its significance for their own modes of production and reception, particularly in a period when art is having to defend its position in the curriculum not only on intrinsic but extrinsic grounds. For example, it cannot be argued that the primacy afforded texts by iconography provides a suitable method to prepare pupils for the semic landscape of today's multi-media arts and communications which no longer attribute to the word a beginning.

The implications here for the relationship between verbal/visual modes of communication and power are touched on by Kress and Leeuwen (1996):

> *The opposition to the emergence of a new visual literacy is not based on an opposition to the visual media as such, but on an opposition to the visual media in situations where they form an alternative to writing and can therefore be seen as a potential threat to the present dominance of verbal literacy among elite groups.*[29]

The authors' 'grammar of visual design' is a systematic and exacting semiotic method for the analysis of images, largely two dimensional, from western culture. It would take too long here to examine the benefits and pitfalls of their system in relation to its application to the classroom, but it undoubtedly provides art and design teachers with a theoretical basis to develop an understanding of visual meaning making. Like any grammar it aims to establish patterns of use, if not exactly rules, and teachers may be wary of any such exercise that aims to define and thus limit and control. However, the authors contend that it is disempowering to deny pupils critical access to the dominant modes of communication. Building on the inclusive visual field embraced by Barthes[30] the authors construct a method for analysing the production of meaning in images concentrating on their formal as opposed to lexical components. However, in place of formalist insularity they 'provide inventories of the major compositional structures which have become established as conventions,' and, following the principles established by the psychologist Arnheim, 'analyse how they are used to produce meaning …'[31] For Kress and Leeuwen, unlike Saussure, signs are never arbitrary but always motivated. Although the motivated sign bears some resemblance to the notion of intention already criticised, for the authors signs are only interesting as a means of 'social (inter)action' not 'self-expression.' It is the use of images, not their intrinsic properties, that is the target of their method, an emphasis that provides a critique of much art and design practice in schools and one that is surely a key factor in any programme that seeks to educate the individual in a social context.

As well as providing art educators with a method to engage pupils in the social, interactive potential of art, semiotics provides ways of examining the relationship between word, image, sound and the other sensory modes used simultaneously in multi-media and installation. Rather than force the visual into the straitjacket of linguistic terminology recent semiotics provides a cross-modal vocabulary: 'it liberates the analyst from the problem that transferring concepts from one discipline into another entails.'[32] Art education does not possess a discrete formal language and teachers are fooling themselves if they think they have not already had recourse to the metaphoric application of others' terms; tone, rhythm, harmony, and metaphor itself, all have their origin in other arts. Semiotics can thus provide a common critical language with which to address not only the relationship between objects and their contexts, but the problematic relationship between objects and their viewing subjects:

> *The idea of 'context' as that which will, in a legislative sense, determine the contours of the work in question is therefore different from the 'context' that semiotics proposes: what the latter points to is, on the one hand, the unarrestable mobility of the signifier, and on the other, the construction of the work of art within always specific contexts of viewing.*[33]

If modernists, artists and educators, have tried to limit the arts by separating them into discrete 'areas of competence … unique to the nature of its medium'[i] they have not done so without forming equivalent definitions of excellence across the arts. The postmodern art educator might consider a different alliance, one in which the key criterion is not quality, and its concomitant genius, but interest achieved in and through diversity: semiotics seeks out qualities of significance not significant quality. In this way the curriculum does not have to be based on hierarchical constructs of worth with their territorial claims and value oppositions but on motivated inquiry, a plural and critical approach to visual culture and its contexts including the pupils' own.

Notes and References

1. Whannel, P. in Chandler, D. [2002] *Semiotics the Basics*. London: Routledge, p. 14.

2. Addison, N. [2003] 'Iconoscepticism: the Value of Images in Education' in N. Addison and L. Burgess (eds.) *Issues in Art and Design Teaching*. London: Routledge.

3. Freedman, K. [1997] 'Teaching Technology for Meaning,' *Art Education 50*, 4, p. 7. Freedman refers to Brown, N. [1989] 'The Myth of Visual Literacy,' *Australian Art Education*, 13 (2) 28–32.

4. Sturrock, J. [1993] *Structuralism*. London: Fontana, pp. 71–73.

5. Bal, M. and Bryson, N. [1991] 'Semiotics and Art History: A Discussion of Context and Senders,' in D. Preziosi (ed.) *The Art of Art History: A Critical Anthology*. Oxford: Oxford University Press, p. 247.

6. Usher, R. and Edwards, E. [1994] *Postmodernism and Education*. London: Routledge, pp. 172–173.

7. Ibid.

8. Foster, H. [1996] *The Return of the Real*, Cambridge. Massachusetts & London: MIT Press, p. xi.

9. Sturrock, J. [1993] *Structuralism*. London: Fontana, p. 73.

10. Thistlewood, D. [1989] *Critical Studies in Art and Design Education*. Burnt Mill: Longman.

11. Davies, T. [1995] *Playing the System*, Birmingham: UCE; Addison, N., Asbury, M., Chittenden, T., De Souza, P. , Georgaki, M., Hulks, D., Papazafiriou, G., Perret, C. and Trowell, J. [2003] *Art Critics and Art Historians in Schools: A Synoptic Report of an Interdisciplinary Research Project*, London: Institute of Education; Steers, J. [2003] 'Art and design in the UK: the theory gap,' in N. Addison and L. Burgess (eds.) *Issues in Art and Design Teaching*, London: Routledge/Falmer.

12. QCA [1998] 'A Survey of Artists, Craftspeople and Designers Used in Teaching Art Research' in *Analysis of Educational Resources in 1997/98*, research coordinated by Clements, R. [1996–97] CENSAPE: University of Plymouth.

13. Dyson, T. [1989] 'Art History in Schools,' in Thistlewood, D. (ed.) *Critical Studies in Art and Design Education*, Burnt Mill: Longman, pp. 130–131; Taylor, B. [1989] 'Art History in the Classroom: a Plea for Caution,' in Thistlewood, D.(ed.) *Critical Studies in Art and Design Education*, Burnt Mill: Longman, pp. 38–39; Parsons, M. J. [1989] *How We Understand Art*, Cambridge: Cambridge University Press; Csikszentmihalyi, M. and Robinson, R. [1990] *The Art of Seeing: An Interpretation of the Aesthetic Experience*, Malibu: J Paul Getty Museum, Getty Centre for Education in the Arts; Schofield, K. [1995] 'Objects of Desire: By Design,' in Prentice, R. (ed.) *Teaching Art and Design*, London: Cassell, pp. 68–79; Cunliffe, L. [1996] 'Art and World View: Escaping the Formalist Labyrinth,' *Journal of Art & Design Education*, 15 (3), Oxford: Blackwell; Dawtrey, L., Jackson, T., Masterson, M., Meecham, P. (eds.) [1996] *Critical Studies and Modern Art*, Milton Keynes: Open University Press, and Addison, N. [2001] 'Tried and Tested: resourceful art histories in art education,' *Engage 8,* London: Engage.

14. Wolfflin, H. [1915] *Principles of Art History*, 6th edition trans. Hottinger, M. [1960] New York.

15. Panofsky, E. [1955] *Meaning in the Visual Arts*, (1983) edition. Middlesex: Penguin.

16. Steinberg, L. [1996] 2nd edition *The Sexuality of Christ in Renaissance Art and in Modern Oblivion*. Chicago and London: The University of Chicago Press.

17. Tickner, L. [2003] 'A Strange Alchemy: Cornelia Parker,' *Art History*, 26 (3). Oxford: Blackwell, pp. 364–391.

18. Ibid. p. 369.

19. Ibid. p. 370.

20. Bal, M. and Bryson, N. [1991] 'Semiotics and Art History: A Discussion of Context and Senders,' in Preziosi, D. (ed.) [1998] *The Art of Art History: A Critical Anthology*. Oxford: Oxford University Press, p. 243.

21. Puttfarken, [1998] "Caravaggio's 'Story of St. Matthew': A challenge to the conventions of painting," *Art History*, 21 (2). Oxford: Blackwell.

22. Ibid. p 177.

23. Holly, M. [1984] *Panofsky and the Foundations of Art History*. New York: Ithaca.

24. Preziosi, D. [1989] *Rethinking Art History*. New Haven & London: Yale University Press, pp. 81–87.

25. Damisch, H. [1975] in Preziosi, D. (ed.) [1998] *The Art of Art History: A Critical Anthology*. Oxford: Oxford University Press, p. 236.

26. Levi-Strauss, C. [1963] 'Do Dual Organisations Exist?' in *Structural Anthropology*, Middlesex: Penguin.

27. Fernie, E. [1995] *Art History and its Methods*. London: Phaidon, p. 127.

28. Damisch, H. [1975] in D. Preziosi (ed.) [1998] *The Art of Art History: A Critical Anthology*. Oxford: Oxford University Press, p. 237.

29. Kress, G. and Leeuwen, T. [1996] *Reading Images: The Grammar of Visual Design*. London: Routledge, p. 16.

30. Barthes, R. [1957] *Mythologies*, (1990 edition) trans, Lavers, A & Smith, C. London: Jonathan Cape.

31. Kress, G. and Leeuwen, T. [1996] *Reading Images: The Grammar of Visual Design*. London: Routledge, p. 1.

32. Bal, M. and Bryson, N. [1991] 'Semiotics and Art History: A Discussion of Context and Senders' in Preziosi, D. (ed.) [1998] *The Art of Art History: A Critical Anthology*. Oxford: Oxford University Press, p. 246.

33. Ibid. p. 252.

34. Greenberg, C. [1965] 'Modernist Painting' in Frascina, F. and Harrison, C. [1982] *Modern Art and Modernism*. London: Paul Chapman Publishing and the Open University.

Originally published in the *Journal of Art & Design Education*, volume 18 (1) 1999.

Chapter 11: On Sampling the Pleasures of Visual Culture: Postmodernism and Art Education

Robin Marriner

I want to explore two issues from ideas about the postmodern that seem to me to raise problems about the practices of art education. Presently I feel more confident that there are difficulties here that need to be addressed than I do about knowing how practice should be redrawn to meet them. First, I want to briefly discuss post-structuralist accounts of meaning and their implications for our concept of the art work as 'object of experience,' 'object of study,' or 'object of knowledge.' Secondly, I want to discuss something which, though separate, has some connection: namely the fairly ubiquitous claim (though with differing value judgments attached), that one of the significant features of the postmodern, and therefore of our present condition, is the erosion or effacement of difference between what has formerly been deemed high and low cultures.

A. Post-structuralist theories of meaning

A1. The relationship between post-structuralism and postmodernism is evidently contentious. Where Jameson's characterisation of the postmodern seems in part constructed from annotating certain facets of post-structuralist thinking, for example, the notion of the 'subject,' and the concept of the 'real,'[1] Huyssen argues that 'we must begin to entertain the notion that rather than offering a theory of postmodernity and developing an analysis of contemporary culture, French theory provides us primarily with an archaeology of modernity, a theory of modernity at the stage of its exhaustion.'[2] Perhaps we can say that if not offering a theory of the postmodern, post-structuralism offers an epistemology which is inconsistent with, or oppositional to the epistemological commitments that underpin modernist culture, and in particular modernist art culture. To that degree it seems, that if not a theory of postmodernism it is profoundly imbricated in what we understand by it.

A2. What is of particular relevance here both to an understanding of postmodern art practice and its implications for art education is the manner in which post-structuralist accounts of meaning run contrary to those to which modernism has covertly, or more recently overtly, had an allegiance.

Within philosophical aesthetics, within art criticism, within art education, our thinking has been traditionally structured by certain oppositions: oppositions for example, between the object and its context; between that which is interior to it and that, exterior; between that which is essential to its meaning and that which is only contingent. Though we have different accounts of what the relationship between the interior and the exterior might be – in some cases that the latter doesn't count at all (for example, formalism), in others that it is heavily determining (for example, the social history of art) – in all such accounts our thinking has already posited or assumed the intelligibility of the concept of an object that exists in separation from that which 'surrounds' or can be brought to it. It is the legitimacy of this assumption that in their different ways, for example, Foucault in his discussion of the 'objects of discourse,' and Derrida in his discussion of the 'parergon' put into question.[3] Both in effect show how that which we take or posit as 'exterior' to the object is a *sine qua non* of the object's visibility and intelligibility to us; that which we take as contingently related to the object is necessarily related to it and in that respect not exterior to our conception of the object at all.

To try and make this more concrete, and at the same time underscore its difference from modernist ideas, I want to look at one example of an argument in support of the autonomy of art works.

The concept of the totally self-sufficient and/yet meaningful art work perhaps received its most rigorous articulation in American art practice and criticism of the Sixties, here I am thinking particularly of the criticism of Michael Fried and Don Judd. Though at the time the latter thought himself to be marking out ground in opposition to Fried's modernist notion of 'presentness' through his concept of 'literalness,' retrospectively the consensus is that he was working within a modernist paradigm.[4] In his essay 'Specific Objects,' Judd elaborates on and secures our understanding of the particular nature of the work he is promoting (in essence minimalist sculpture) through distinguishing it from what it is not: its 'literalness' is spelt out in terms of its being non-illusionistic, non-allusionistic, non-referential, non-representational, etc.[5] 'Literal' is also used within the text to signify that the meaning of the object is given by or consists in just *what is there*: the obdurate

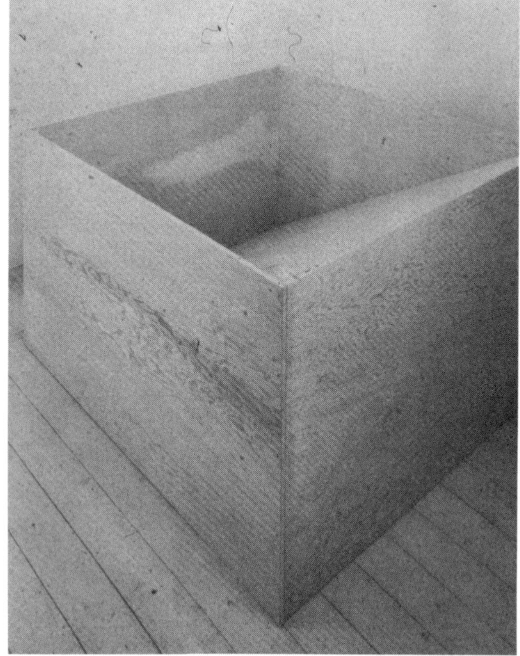

Untitled *1974 by Don Judd, Plywood 36x60x60 ins*

thing, its materials, the simple relation of its parts, etc. These two uses are taken as equivalent or synonymous to underpin that '… only what can be seen is there … What you see is what you see.'[6] At first glance, in fact at several glances, given how long these ideas have had a currency in the art world, a convincing case seems to be made for the idea of an object that is totally self-sufficient and meaningful: it is self-referential, literally 'just what it is,' and declares that.

That there is a problem lurking here can be brought out if we remind ourselves that there is a perfectly legitimate way of describing what we *literally* see when we look at a Judd work as a plywood box of certain dimensions with a recessed edge, or say in the case of an Andre, a pile of one hundred and twenty fire bricks in a certain arrangement. This is not of course what Judd means when he says of the object that it is literal, that its meaning is given by what is literally there, for Judd is not talking about objects that are (simply) plywood boxes or piles of bricks but about objects that are art. The difficulty is that in the sense in which being made of plywood is a literal property of the object, literally visible and amenable to sight (which is what the persuasiveness of the argument hangs on), it seems to me that the artness isn't. If we see the plywood box, or see the pile of bricks but are unable to see the art, there is nothing more to see, there is no further literal property that we have overlooked that is going to make visible its artness. In order to 'see' the sculpture what we need is something that is precisely not given in the literal/visible properties of the object: we need a familiarity with other objects, values and

Equivalent V111 *1968 by Carl Andre, Fire bricks*

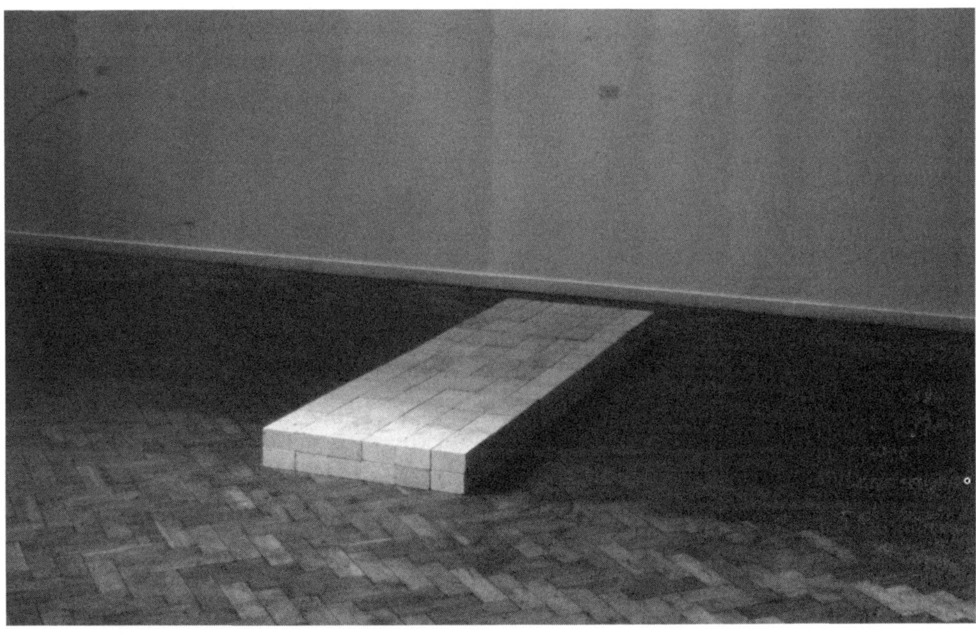

knowledges, only in relation to which do the 'literal' properties take on the meaning of art. One might say it is only because these relations are put into play within Judd's text, (e.g. we know what it is for something to be' 'non-illusionistic'), but are not overtly acknowledged, that the idea of an object that has no relations and is meaningful gains any credence and seems to become intelligible to us. One might go further and say that though when we perceive the object (simply) as a physical object, a plywood box, the relations of which I speak are exterior to the object and contingent, in so far as the object is perceived and experienced as a work of art those relations are absolutely necessary; without them the object which is the object of art, the aesthetic would not come into being. In so far as that is persuasive, those relations are then not contingently related and exterior to the object but interior and constitutive of it.[7]

In a large nutshell I am suggesting that theories of autonomy in relation to artworks are highly problematic if we accept a post-structuralist account of meaning. Despite the differences (that in this context I have chosen to ignore) between thinkers designated as poststructuralists, they have in common a shared acceptance of two of the fundamental propositions put forward by de Saussure, namely, that a sign comes into being *qua* sign, i.e., means, in virtue of its relation to and difference from other signs within a system; secondly, that the relationship between the elements of a sign, between a signifier and a signified is not natural and motivated but arbitrary and conventional. Though post-structuralists differ from Saussure and structuralists in their rejection of the weight that the latter give to the system, ('langue') as the object of study, they all have in common the belief that *meaning is relational*. Theories that meaning can be inherent, immanent or present in/to the sign are cast as untenable because they have misconstrued the logical conditions under which meaning can transpire.

A3. One educational implication of this seems to me to be for what has to be included within the 'object of study' when we are studying art objects. If, as was claimed above the 'work of art' as an 'object of experience,' or an 'object of criticism' only comes into being in its relations, then those relations are not contingent but (logically) necessary to both its ontological status and its meaning. If we allow that 'theory' can be taken as equivalent to having epistemological commitments or allegiances, (rather than overt theorising), then it follows that theory is always at work in the 'work' *qua* 'work of art,' or the 'object' *qua* 'object of criticism.' There is no 'work of art' without theory being at work, and no 'object of criticism' without theory. (To claim the former, it should be stressed, is not equivalent to claiming or implying that all art works are overtly 'theoretical' or concerned with their own ontological status). It would seem to me that theory therefore has to be included in an art education that is to give an understanding of and access to how works mean.

Another implication of the above is that if something takes on the status of 'art work' and signifies meaning *qua* art work in virtue of its relations, then those relations are productive in generating that art work in its specificity – as that kind of object meaning this, e.g., Andre's 'Equivalence No 8.' We need to reflect further on now these relations come to pass. Rather than see talking about art, writing about art, and the other modes through which we approach and present art to ourselves as in some way mediating or translating or making 'available' an anterior formed (and in respect of meaning 'complete') object, we have to acknowledge the performative aspects of our activities. In the acts of speaking, writing, presenting slides, hanging work we are placing or locating that on which we act, we are generating relations through which the art object in its specificity is produced. (One might say the artist does the same.)[8] This seems to me unavoidable, the problem is that rarely in any of the areas in which art is engaged or studied is it presently acknowledged. (I'm sure we all could cite innumerable talks, lectures, exhibition guides, catalogues, journal articles, etc., wherein, under the guise of an exclusive concern to present the meaning of work, certain relations are taken as already in place but not 'spoken': that is, a 'placing' of the work for the student/reader/viewer is effected by presenting to the student/reader/viewer a work that has already been 'placed' in relation to a body of knowledge or theory.) What in part needs consideration and further examination is the possible ways in which relations can be generated and put in place if certain kinds of experience are to become available/accessible … but at least as importantly, that in our making of claims about the meaning of works we disclose that it is always in relation to some body of knowledge that they are being made: that that knowledge is itself declared.

It seems to me that art education, criticism, shows/exhibitions cannot themselves guarantee that certain experiences will happen, nor can they (ever) offer a definitive meaning of works; relations can always change both across time and different audiences. A defensible characterisation of education, criticism and exhibition culture has to recognise that conditionality, that though my not having an experience or not perceiving meanings posited by a particular critical practice can come about through my lack of awareness of the relations and knowledges that the practice aspires to put in place, equally they can come about through a refusal of those relations and knowledges in favour of my commitment to others. Embracing particular experiences and meanings in relation to an art work always involves embracing far more than is overtly on offer. Though art culture too often operates like a 'Goodfella,' if not on pain of death, at least of social exclusion, it doesn't make an offer that can't be refused.

B. High/low culture

B. The second thing I wanted to explore briefly is the purported collapse of the boundary between high and popular or mass culture, which is seen as a characteristic of postmodernism.

B1. For example Jameson:

The second feature of this list of postmodernism is the effacement in it of some key boundaries or separations, most noticeably the erosion of the older distinction between high culture and so-called mass or popular culture. This is perhaps the most distressing development of all from an academic standpoint, which has traditionally had a vested interest in preserving a realm of high or elite culture against the surrounding environment of philistinism, of schlock and kitsch, of TV series and Readers Digest culture, in transmitting difficult and complex skills of reading, listening and seeing to its initiates.[9]

Or, for example, Lyotard when contrasting the effects of ideological prescriptions for culture under Stalinism and Fascism with that of recent capitalist culture, of the latter says:

When power is that of capital and not that of the party, the 'transavantgardist' or 'postmodern' (in Jencks's sense) solution proves to be the better adapted to than the anti-modern solution. Eclecticism is the degree zero of contemporary general culture: one listens to reggae, watches a western, eats McDonald's food for lunch and local cuisine for dinner, wears Parisian perfume in Tokyo and 'retro' clothes in Hong Kong; knowledge is a matter of TV games. It is easy to find a public for eclectic works. By becoming kitsch, art panders to the confusion which reigns in the 'taste' of the patrons. Artists, gallery owners, critics, and public wallow together in the 'anything goes' and the epoch is one of slackening.[10]

Where eclecticism and its incumbent 'slackening' is seen as art lowering itself into the value realm of the popular.

Or finally Huyssen, where something of this purported change is intimated in the book's title *After the Great Divide: Modernism, Mass Culture and Postmodernism*, and further elaborated within:

The postmodern sensibility of our time is different from both modernism and avant-gardism precisely in that it raises the question of cultural tradition and conservation in the most fundamental way as an aesthetic and political issue … my main point about contemporary postmodernism is that it operates in a field of tension between tradition and innovation, conservation and renewal, mass culture and high art, in which the second terms are no longer automatically privileged over the first.[11]

B2. From an art culture perspective, the above seems to be less true than is claimed. Though there is evidence that the relationship between some art culture and popular or mass culture has perhaps undergone a change, I can think of no recent work that engages with popular culture that presents itself or declares itself as anything other than art. It is situated in galleries and other art institutions, written about principally in art journals, (and when written about elsewhere – in style or fashion magazines – is always written about as art), and is made by people who pursue/demand recognition as artists.

As John Roberts has remarked in relation to Young British Artists:

> *The new generation of British artists (with) their privileged exposure in the Eighties to the systematic incorporation of contemporary art theory and philosophy into art education have possibly been the first to recognise ... what was needed to move art onwards generationally. It would be mistaken to identify the new art and its fuck-you attitudinising with anything as simple-minded as the 'depoliticisation' of art. Despite much of the new art's unqualified regard for the voluptuous pleasures of popular culture (drug references and experiences and the arcana of tabloid TV being common denominators) it does not seek to assimilate itself to popular culture in fazed admiration.[12]*

What is perhaps different about much art that has had a high visibility in the past fifteen or so years is that it no longer seems to locate itself either in the position of critical opposition to or critical disengagement from popular culture, (or at least not in the sense that we are used to understanding that). That is, it seems to refuse the positions most commonly conceptualized within modernism (that of the Frankfurt School or of the Greenberg model) as to art's relation to the popular. Not surprisingly in certain circles this has been perceived as the relinquishing of art's radical heritage, of its absorption into the market (for example, on the one side by the likes of Kuspit and Gablik, on the other Buchloh). However, it is possible to give an alternative reading which suggests that what is being rejected or challenged is certain Modernists' conception of popular or mass culture, i.e., certain concepts of art's 'other.' This would be less to challenge that much mass culture is produced for the orchestration and regulation of needs and desires supportive of capitalism but that that culture is necessarily as unproblematically consumed as the accepted narratives have said. Here the difference might be seen in the shift between say the work of Burgin and Prince [Illustrations 3 and 4] and the respective ways in which they treat, and position, us in relation to the Marlboro images that they 'represent.' What in part at least seems to be at issue here is the idea that the commodification of an object precludes its having critical or radical effects. Or that the condition of being radical is dependent upon the eluding of the commodity form. Much art of the past fifteen or so years (and like many other recent preoccupations this can been seen as prefigured in Warhol's work) seems to have rejected the modernist tenet that the commodity form can be eluded – i.e., to have relinquished that as a myth about art's status – and begun its investigations from the basis of that not being the case.

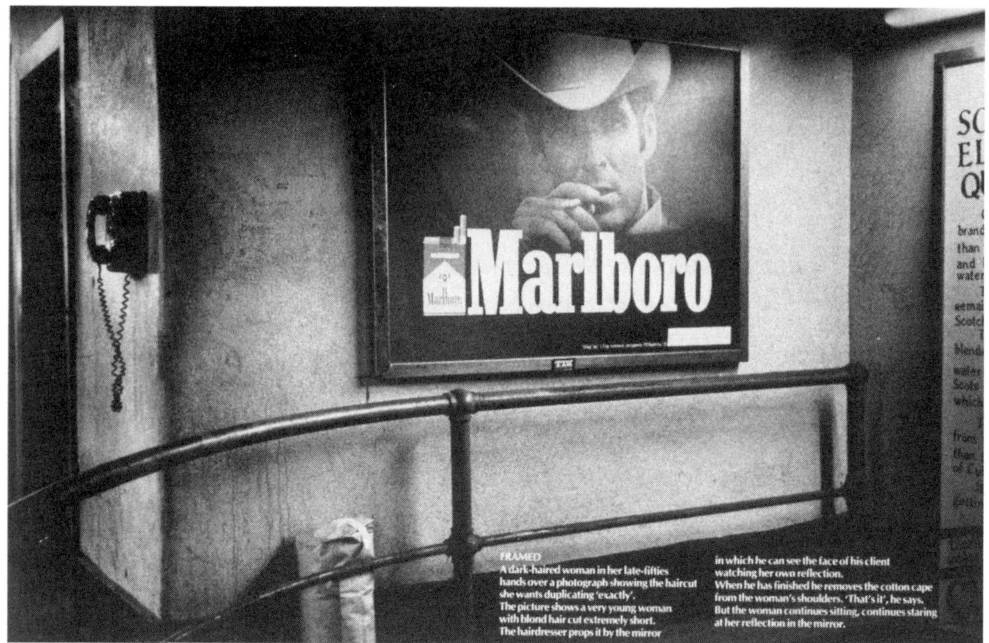

US 77 *(one of 12 panels) by Victor Burgin, 40x 60 ins 1977*

Untitled Cowboys, *1968, by Richard Prince*

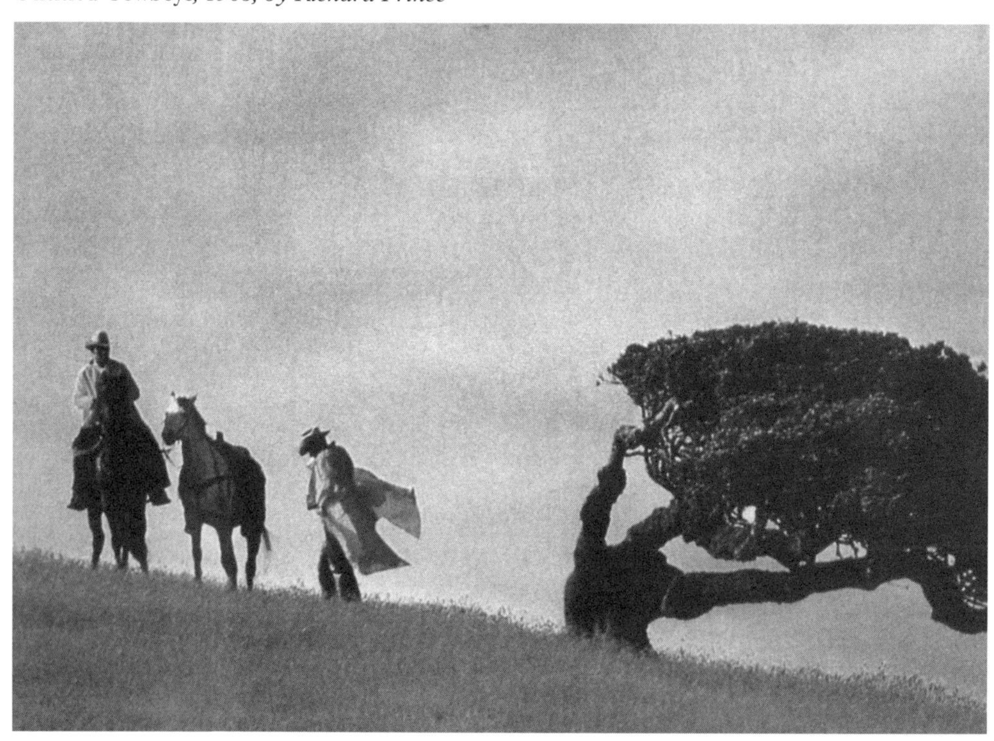

More profoundly perhaps, much art can be read as either interrogating or rejecting the grounds on which the distinction between art objects and the objects of popular culture within modernism are made. From a certain perspective again this might be read as the collapse of distinctions or difference, (by those with an allegiance to modernism), but from elsewhere it can be read as an exploration or examination of where the grounds for that distinction are to be located. Koons' and Steinbach's work, for example – again, neither of whom would see themselves as other than artists – could be seen as addressing the social constructedness of those distinctions, as locating them not as an intrinsic, immanent quality of the object/work itself, as would be narrated within or assumed by modernist epistemology, but rather as in the relations between the objects and the discursive and institutional realms within which they are placed and circulated.[13]

It is perhaps here that the two issues with which this paper started begin to interconnect. Not, as it may sound, because I want to suggest that many recent works can be read as illustrations or embodiments of post-structuralist theory, but rather because if read in relation to post-structuralist theory the works appear less as backsliding or inadequate than intelligible as rejecting or challenging modernist assumptions. In so far as postmodernism can be understood as involving an epistemological shift from modernism, to that degree can the works be designated as postmodern. (In fact there is evidence that many of the artists who became visible in the 80s, e.g., Kruger, Prince, Steinbach, Salle, Sherman had a familiarity with recent theory.)

Of course, it's not just post-structuralists that have overtly theorised the issue of demarcating art and accounted for it as other than in the object. Despite their mutual recriminations, Danto,[14] and Bourdieu[15] have enough in common with each other and with what I am trying to suggest that they could have been recruited to give some support.

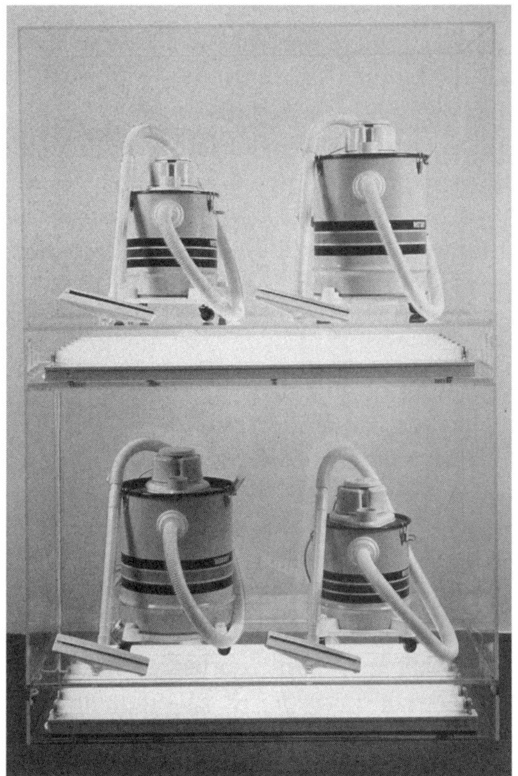

New Shelton Wet/Dry Doubledecker,
1981, by Jeff Koons

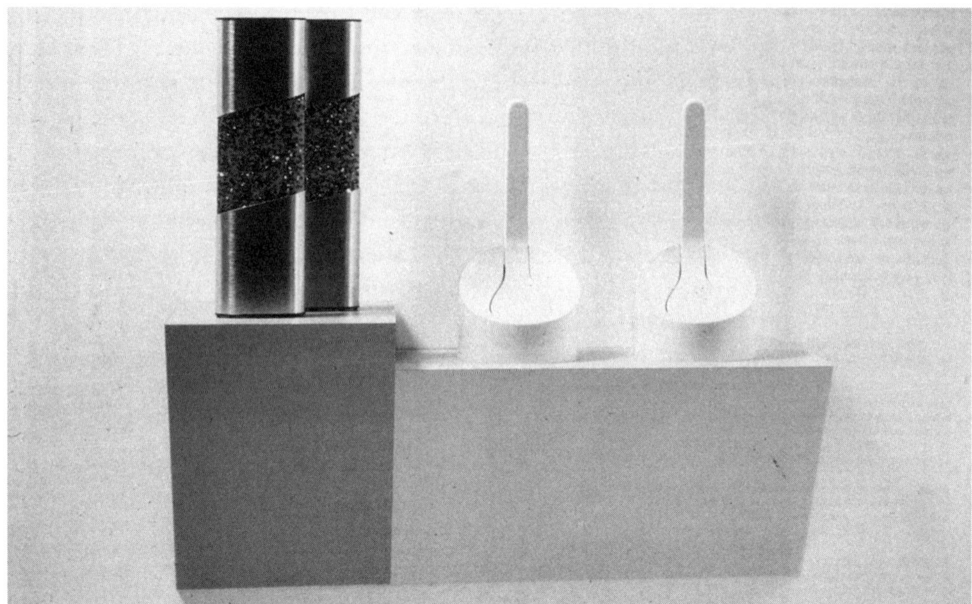

Security and Serenity *by Haim Steinbach*

In short, I am trying to suggest that the implications of present theory around art, and the present practice of art are not that the boundaries within the culture have collapsed (though for some both the theory and the practice are perceived to have such implications, e.g., Herwitz on Danto: 'the concept of pictorial object reduces to the concept of a mere conventional sign in the theoretical commerce of the world, to be variously interpreted at will,'[16] or, for example *Modern Painters* or Giles Auty or Brian Sewell on practice), but rather in theory and in practice the grounds for making that distinction have been relocated. This seems to me to have implications for art education:

First, we cannot assume that an understanding of and the experiencing of the pleasures of art culture can be privileged above an understanding of and the pleasures of other aspects of (visual) culture. Of the possible reactions to this perhaps the most obvious are: we should study visual culture rather than art or that we should study art but have to justify it on grounds other than its inherent superiority. If nothing else it suggests an area that requires further address.

Secondly, despite what Herwitz says (above), the position argued here doesn't mean that what we call interpretation can happen at will. Rather in order for something to count as an 'interpretation' already positions it as intelligible in relation to an established body/field of knowledge. To become a member of that 'interpretive community,' [Fish] one has to be an initiate to that knowledge. In effect every time we 'read' something we are privileging certain knowledges, which means there are also always (some group's) values at work. I have tried to suggest that presently this is more often than not in denial in art cultural practice – what is presently covert should be made overt.

Thirdly, we might say that, to an extent, different knowledges are put into play in approaching art works, (from within art culture) than are put into play in our approaching the works of popular culture. (This is not to suggest a rigid mutual exclusivity, or even anything as rigid as sometimes Bourdieu seems to be suggesting – popular cultural objects often draw upon and play with knowledges from art culture and vice-versa, but rather that to perceive something *qua* art object necessitates certain knowledges of the 'field'). Within what I am trying to argue about the postmodern, differences are acknowledged (the distinction has not been effaced). What has been relinquished is the assumption of a hierarchy in that difference. (For example, Koons on the fetishisation of 'newness' in the art world and in commodity culture in the New Show).

An argument for Art Education could be one for getting certain knowledges (i.e., those different from the better circulated knowledges necessary for an understanding of the popular) circulated in order that the meanings of art culture can be assessed and its pleasures embraced or rejected from a position of choice. As I suggested above, experiences can't be guaranteed to happen. Though I'm no longer confident of the superiority of art culture's pleasures over other pleasures, they are pleasures that I would not want to do without. If nothing else, art culture certainly enhances the range of pleasures available to us – given the condition under which many of us have to live our lives that seems no bad thing.

Notes and References

1. Jameson, F. [1984] 'Postmodernism: Cultural Logic of Late Capitalism,' *New Left Review*, 146, July/August.

2. Huyssen, A. [1986] 'Mapping the Postmodern' in *After the Great Divide*. Macmillan, p. 209.

3. Foucault, M. [1974] *The Archaeology of Knowledge*, Tavistock Publications, pp. 40–9; Derrida, J. [1987] *The Truth in Painting*. (Trans. Bennington and McLeod), Chicago: University of Chicago Press. See particularly pp. 60–1.

4. See for example, Krauss, R. [1977] *Passages in Modern Sculpture*, MIT Press, Cambridge, MA and Foster, H. [1986] The Crux of Minimalism, in *Individuals: a Selected History of Contemporary Art 1945–1986*, Los Angeles: MOCA.

5. Judd, D. [1965] 'Specific Objects' in *Arts Yearbook* No 8. Reprinted in Don Judd [1975] *Complete Writings 1959–1975*. Press of Nova Scotia College, and New York Press.

6. Stella, F. [1966] in 'Questions of Stella and Judd,' Bruce Glaser, *Art News*, September. Reprinted in Battcock, G. [1968] *Minimal Art: a critical reader*. Dutton and Co. NY, p. 158.

7. For a more detailed and thorough examination of Derrida's ideas and their implications for our understanding of 'art objects' see my, 'Derrida and the Parergon' in Smith, P. and Wilde, C. (eds.) [2002] *A Companion to Art Theory*. Oxford: Blackwells.

8. This is not to deny artistic agency but rather to suggest that it cannot itself be understood in separation from 'theory': that the notion of an agency or intention that is 'artistic' is not intelligible in separation from particular relations.

9. Jameson F. [1985] 'Postmodernism and Consumer Society' in Foster H. (ed.) *Postmodern Culture*. Pluto Press, p. 112.

10. Lyotard J-F. 'Answering the Question: What is Postmodernism?' in Lyotard J-F. [1979/84] *The Postmodern Condition: a Report on Knowledge*. Manchester University Press, p. 76.

11. Huyssen A. [1988] *After the Great Divide: Modernism, Mass culture and Postmodernism*. Macmillan, p. 217.

12. Roberts J. [1996] 'Mad for it. Philistinism, the Everyday, and New British Art,' *Third Text*, 35, summer (my emphasis).

13. For more substantial support see my, 'Signs of the Times: Sculpture as Non-Specific Objects: the work of Koons and Steinbach,' *Art Monthly*. No 138. July/Aug 1990.

14. Danto, A. [1981] *The Transfiguration of the Common Place*. Harvard University Press.

15. Bourdieu, P. [1993] *The Field of Cultural Production*. Polity Press. In relation to Danto, see especially 'The Historical Genesis of the Pure Aesthetic.'

16. Herwitz, D. [1993] *Making Theory Constructing Art*. University of Chicago, p. 203.

Originally published in the *Journal of Art & Design Education*, volume 18 (1) 1999.

Chapter 12: A Critical Reading of the National Curriculum for Art in the Light of Contemporary Theories of Subjectivity

Dennis Atkinson

Introduction

Contemporary theory in the social sciences describes how subjectivity is constituted within specific practices and discourses. These discursive practices produce knowledges which identify individuals and their abilities. Under the gaze of pedagogic discourses and practices pupils' abilities become visible, are constituted, sanctioned or corrected. Under this gaze pupils are defined as learners. This paper is concerned with how pupils are constructed as learners within the English Art National Curriculum. The paper is in three parts. In part one, a brief description of theories of subjectivity and discourse is provided from the work of Foucault and Lacan. In part two, central ideas from the theory are applied to show how assessment in the National Curriculum for art invokes a particular construction of practice in which pupils' ability is defined. In part three, an alternative way is offered for conceiving practice grounded in the idea of difference.

Part 1: Theorising subjectivity: Foucault

In much contemporary social and cultural theory the term 'subjectivity' is used to refer to how we are constituted as social subjects. That is to say it refers to how our understanding of ourselves and others is formed. We tend to think of ourselves as people whose thoughts and actions are largely self-propelled and that truths about the world can be discovered though rational thought. For example, expression and representation in art practice are often viewed as the products of original thought and action. These processes are often identified by the term 'self-expression.'

Foucault[1] devoted much of his time to studying how subjectivities are formed, how we become subjects, within social formations. Essentially he argued that much of our understanding of ourselves and others is produced in particular sites of practice within institutions such as schools. These institutions promote particular forms of practice and language (discourse) in which understanding is constituted. Individuals become visible to themselves and to others through the terms of such institutional practices and discourses. The key idea is that such practices and discourses construct rather than discover who we are. The idea of a fully constituted self which exists prior to discourse therefore becomes problematic. Foucault formulates a subject which is determined by the social order, that is to say a subject who is constructed, regulated and *made visible as a subject* within institutional and other social apparatuses. My concern here is to consider how pupils or teachers become visible through the discursive practices which constitute the pedagogic encounter in the teaching of art in schools.

A pupil's ability in drawing practice, for example, is not to be viewed as an inherent capacity which can be liberated or discovered (even though we may think this to be the case), but as constituted within particular sites of teaching practice and their corresponding discourses, of representation for example. These, through their particular regimes of knowledge, constitute and regulate aspects of subjectivity such as drawing ability.

The pupil is 'subjected' to the gaze of a particular knowledge discourse through which the pupil's ability is measured or categorised. Within such practices and discourses pupils are constituted as powerful (able) or not (less able). Usher & Edwards refer to the concealed nature of power imbued in discourse in the following way:

> *Power-knowledge, formations operate through the practices which inscribe the person as a particular subject prior to entering an educational institution and those practices they are engaged in once within it; in becoming a subject' we learn to be a 'subject' of 'a particular sort. It is our assumptions about the nature of the subject' which then inform our practices as teachers and learners, yet the effect of power which gives rise to the particular positioning of subjects is effectively veiled.*[2]

Lacan, the symbolic order and points-de-capiton

Lacan[3] also theorises the human subject as being formed within the symbolic order. This is his term for the entire symbolic network occurring within a social formation. Language is primary within the symbolic order but it is also composed of other symbolic practices such as visual codes of representation, customs and rituals.

In their discussion of Lacanian psychoanalysis and education, Usher and Edwards[4] identify pedagogic discourses as structuring and positioning learners in schools. Pupils are woven into specific curriculum practices through 'master signifiers' and their respective discourses which structure pupil subjectivities, in terms, for example, of ability. These master signifiers correspond to the Lacanian *points de capiton*,[5] which operate through a process of stitching pupils into the discourse through key signifiers by which their identity as learners is constructed. Coward and Ellis[6] describe *points de capiton* as 'privileged points at which the direction of the signifying chain is established.' To illustrate how this stitching process operates in discourse in order to constitute pupils' drawing ability, consider the following transcription from a video in which teachers are asked to consider two drawings. This is what they say about the more successful drawing:

better composition …, better structured …, finer balance to it …, more exciting …, it moves you into the picture …, it sits on the paper very well …, more awareness of texture and perspective.[7]

The teachers' comments constitute an assessment of the more successful drawing and, by implication, the weaker drawing. Particular words are used to describe the more successful drawing. The assessment discourse recognises particular formal qualities and thus establishes a powerful inclusory and exclusory classification so that the more successful drawing is viewed as being produced by a more able pupil. Key terms such as 'composition' and 'perspective' stitch the drawing, and the drawer, to a particular representational discourse and practice which possesses a chain and structure of meaning through which identity as a subject of drawing practice is constructed. The discourse imputes the presence of a particular ability. It is through the gaze of the discourse that both the drawing as an object and the pupil as a subject are produced.

Part 2: The National Curriculum for Art, a critical reading

In the National Curriculum for Art[8] the central focus is upon teaching pupils specific skills, practices and bodies of knowledge. Pupils should be taught how to develop both visual perception and visual literacy. They should be taught the relevant skills needed to 'express ideas and feelings' and 'record observations' (visual perception) as well as be taught the different ways in which 'ideas, feelings and meanings are communicated in visual form' (visual literacy).

In order to comment upon this approach to visual perception and visual literacy I will refer to the document *Exemplification of Standards, for Key Stage 3*.[9] This text supplements the National Curriculum for art programmes of study by aiming to promote consistency in teacher assessment of pupils' work. The text constitutes a discourse which articulates a particular construction of ability (subjectivity) and practice. It concentrates upon achievement and progression in pupils' learning in art in relation to particular standards which they are expected to achieve by the end of key stage three. Pupils' work is classified as either working towards, achieving or working beyond particular expectations. In Foucauldian terms these classifications establish a normative discursive regime in which pupils' abilities in art practice are positioned and regulated. Pupils' ability in art is made visible through the terms of the assessment discourse, which articulates a particular construction of practice and ability.

The first series of paintings in the document are chosen to demonstrate assessment of pupils' use of technical and expressive skills in recording ideas and feelings, as well as ability to analyse and represent chosen features of the natural and made environment. Three paintings are selected as outcomes of a project in which pupils are engaged in recording observations of the local environment.

Each painting is assessed using the above-mentioned classification. A common criterion for assessment concerns the pupil's ability to record what is seen accurately:

Painting 1. Information about the shapes of buildings and, machinery which feature in the environment has been observed and recorded but greater analysis is needed in order to represent this accurately.

Painting 2. The shapes of buildings and other objects in the environment have been selected, analysed and represented with some accuracy, technical skill and attention to detail which indicates firsthand observation.

Painting 3. There is a detailed and accurate analysis of the buildings and their surroundings. The shapes of buildings and details of the setting have been selected, recorded and organised into a coherent form.[10]

The term 'accuracy' suggests that it is possible to achieve a representation which mirrors perceptual experience. It invokes a particular discourse in which the paintings become visible and regulated *as practice*. Vision is assumed to be an unmediated experience and the drawing or painting process one in which vision can be recorded, in varying degrees of accuracy. Furthermore vision is assumed to be a universal vision which is universally experienced, and the paintings can be assessed by reference to this universal criterion. Variation in the standards achieved by each pupil is due to their varying ability, within this universal continuum, to observe and then record what is observed. The term 'accurate' suggests that recording what is observed through painting or drawing is perceived as a mirroring process, and assessment seems to be concerned with gauging how closely a particular image approximates the truth of perception.

This key discursive term positions the pupil's practice and thus the pupil's ability within the assessment discourse. In this discourse the pupil becomes visible as a pedagogic subject. The term 'accurate' in Lacanian parlance constitutes the *point de capiton*, around which the assessment discourse is structured. It presupposes an understanding of vision in which a world of extension is reflected through the retinal membrane onto a passive specular consciousness, and an understanding of representation in which the representational image, in varying degrees of success reproduces the retinal image. Pupils' drawings or paintings which do not conform to this form of optical truth are seen either as a consequence of inadequate perception or lack of skill. Thus the pupil becomes visible as a pedagogic subject within a discourse in which vision and representation are given specific constructions. Vision is taken to identify a universal ontological process whilst representation is understood in terms of a simple idea of mimesis.

I would argue that these paintings are not representations of a prior reality, but that they are productions; they bring into the world a semiotic order; these pupils are doing work with visual signs. The paintings are not the result of a universal vision, they are outcomes of local processes of seeing, noticing and constructing. To advocate that these paintings can be assessed as *working towards*, *achieving or working beyond*, a norm of expectation, ignores the legitimacy, coherence and difference of each pupil's local processes of practice.

These differences, I suggest, are embedded within the different semiotic logics which each pupil employs. Such differences reflect each pupil's observing-recording dialectic, which are embedded within each pupil's different noticing-responding practices. These practices are not reducible or assessable according to a universal vision, or a mimetic representation, nor, I believe, to a normative conception of development. To claim that one painting is more advanced than another because it is a more accurate representation or recording of observation is to assume the false premise that an accurate representation is a mirror of the visible, and that vision is an unmediated universal process. Copjec, following Lacan, argues:

> *Semiotics, not optics, is the science that enlightens for us the structure of the visual domain. Because it alone is capable of lending things sense, the signer alone makes vision possible. There is and can be no brute vision, no vision totally independent of language. Painting, drawing, all forms of picture making, then, are fundamentally graphic arts. And because all signifiers are material, that is, because they are opaque rather than translucent, refer to other signifiers rather than directly to a signified, the field of vision is neither clear nor easily traversable.[11]*

And yet the assessment discourse produced to inform assessment of art practice in the National Curriculum, implies that vision is clear and easily traversable. The discourse assumes a clear uncomplicated relation between vision and representation; pupils' paintings are assessed within this discursive relation and the pupils' painting abilities as practice become visible in the discourse. Pupils' differences of painting practice are transformed and reconfigured within the normative structure of the assessment discourse which is given sense by key discursive terms such as 'accuracy.'

Summary

So, what's wrong with the discourse which constitutes the National Curriculum for Art? Well, first of all, it implies an outmoded conceptualisation of practice. For example, vision is assumed to be a universal process and representation is assumed to be a simple mirroring of a prior experiential original. Secondly, it attempts to establish normative frameworks within which practices such as drawing and painting can be assessed. Such frameworks tend to pathologise legitimate personal representational strategies. Thirdly, it suggests that through these normative frameworks pupils' ability in art can be defined and regulated.

The value of exploring the constitution of subjectivity by applying the work of Foucault and Lacan, is that in different ways, they invite us to examine the way in which discourse constructs our understanding of subjectivity rather than revealing it. Foucault shows how institutional discourses, such as the National Curriculum, create normative structures in which subjects are positioned, made visible and regulated. When applied to art practices in schools, it helps us to consider how both teachers and pupils become visible as pedagogic subjects.

The difficulty with this constructivist understanding of subjectivity for art in education is that if we are not careful, the human subject, or human agency, can be left out of the equation altogether! If subjectivity in art practice is understood as shaped entirely by a network of discourses and practices (the social formation), then this ignores the fact that discourses and practices are operated, reviewed and changed by human agents. People do work with discourses and practices. Human subjects and their actions therefore need not only to be understood as constructions of discourse and practice but also as manipulating discourse and practice.

Part 3: Representation, identity and difference: speculations for practice

The increase in the rate of social change includes an interrogation of culture and practice once viewed as fixed and immutable. Such questioning has demonstrated the inadequacy of viewing the human subject as an essential individual. Burgin states:

We become what we are only through our encounter, while growing up, with the multitude of representations of what we may become – the various positions that society allocates to us. There is no essential self which precedes the social construction of the self through the agency of representations.[12]

It is our 'encounter with the multitude of representations,' and 'the various positions that society allocate us,' which suggests a subject who is not pre-constituted, but constituted within, or even between, particular but differing and changing contexts of social practice.

Within the art curriculum, responses to increasing social complexity have involved multi-cultural, anti-racist, and gender initiatives. These have cast a critical spotlight upon traditional practices and forms of representation to challenge curriculum content, practice or representation. The search for visibility between cultures which produced movements such as multi-culturalism or anti-racism in the 1970s and 1980s has shifted towards considering the idea of difference as a multi-layered phenomenon. The idea of cultural hybridity suggests states of flux, fluidity and coalescence which make it difficult to think in terms of cultural origins.

The application of theoretical work concerned with subjectivity or identity to pedagogic practices, sharpens the focus upon the material production of subjects in the curriculum. Such application deconstructs the hegemony of traditional curriculum content and practices and their impact upon learning, but also, crucially, provides the possibility to explore different approaches to teaching and learning and, consequently, to develop a far more inclusive approach to subject constitution in curriculum sites.

I don't believe we can afford to rethink the art curriculum by revisiting questions such as 'what is the nature of art,' 'what is the nature of art in education' or even 'what is the nature of development in practices such as drawing.' Such questions demand essentialist replies which are not compatible with the flux and difference of social formations, or the complex inter-active processes described in contemporary theories of human development and understanding. So how do we rethink or remodel the art curriculum?

Read's[13] influential discussion of the value of art in education was based upon his seduction by popular psychological discourses of the time. It was in terms of such discourses that Read constructed the child as a practitioner of art and this discourse influenced many art educators in their reflections and approaches to practice. In other words they came to think about and construct their practice in terms of the particular discourse popularised by Read.

In the light of my critical reading of the National Curriculum for Art, which discourses are likely to provide a way of conceiving practice which will lead to a re-conceiving of the art curriculum? Discourses concerned with difference, representation and identity may provide a platform for change.

Difference can be employed as a guiding conception for initiating and evaluating art practice in schools. It is a concept which Derrida[14] re-works through the term *différance*, to suggest that meaning is never total, fixed or final, but always fluid and contingent. By combining the terms, to differ and to defer, he claims that meaning is constituted through a differential sequence of signifiers (words or images) which are always open to interpretation. Although contexts or intentions may assert some influence upon meaning they can never completely determine meaning.

It is possible to apply a logic of difference to art practice. In assessing pupils' art practice we need to be aware of the difference between assessment discourse and the pupils' art work. The notion of *différance* implies that the visual image or construction is not absolutely translatable into language, thus requiring a deep respect for the image. This raises questions of relevance in relation to the nature of assessment in art education, for it suggests that there is always something lacking in the assessment discourse *vis a vis* the pupil's practice. We need to be sensitive to the difference between the art work as a construction in discourse and the art work 'in itself,' though we can never articulate this difference! The difficulty lies in the fact that in order to evaluate, to assess, to debate or discuss pupils' art practice we must do so by using categorisations of discourse. Perhaps the difference to which I refer here constitutes an aporia for as long as the practice of assessment remains.

Difference can also relate to the differences between representational practices which pupils employ and the need to acknowledge the legitimacy of such difference. We need to be wary of inclusory and exclusory (hegemonic) effects of discourse when assessing art practices. We require a pedagogical space large enough to accommodate differences of practice, which will enable our responses to different practices of representation to be compatible with such difference. This involves a deep respect for the art work which may challenge the limits of our understanding of practice. In relation to representation this requires understanding vision not as a universal or natural process, but as located within specific ontological spaces which are embedded within transforming cultural and historical traditions.

Difference, representation and identity are conceptual tools for exploring practice in relation to culture and tradition. Contemporary theorisations of these concepts suggest that both culture and identity do not refer to discrete bodies of tradition and practice or discrete identities of individuals. Social formations are transient, involving rapid cultural fusions, hybridities, ephemeral and fluid identities.[15]

In relation to critical and contextual studies, Foucault's work on discourse and power allows us to consider aesthetic discourse, not in terms of discovering the truth or meaning of an art work, but as producing a particular reading embedded within a particular ideology of the subject, representation and practice. Perhaps part of a reconceptualised art curriculum should be concerned with an interrogation of aesthetic discourse itself. Questioning the discourses in which we understand art practice or representation, may help us to see the productive effects of such discourses, revealing their cultural and ideological underpinnings and hegemonies of practice.

Contemporary theorisations of subjectivity describe the productive effects of institutional practices and discourses. They show how what were once understood to be natural processes, for example: ability, vision, development are discursive constructions which provide specific readings of such processes. In some ways this situation creates a lack of certainty when considering the content of an art curriculum because it reveals the ideological basis of practice and representation as well as their cultural and historical underpinnings. If we wish to dehegemonise traditional attitudes to practice and representation for example, how do we proceed to understand practice? For example, how should we understand drawing or painting as practice, how should these practices be taught, how will they be assessed?

In other ways this lack of certainty may provide the opportunity to construct an art curriculum in which ability and practice (pupils' subjectivities) are not understood within narrow normative frameworks. Contemporary theorisations of subjectivity, difference and identity which radicalise our understanding of these issues, provide the opportunity to formulate a curriculum for art in which concepts such as difference and identity challenge us to provide a new framework for practice. A framework which provides a more inclusive and respectful approach to practice, driven by this respect rather than by an assessment structure grounded in a limited conception of practice.

Notes and References

1. Foucault, M. [1979] *Discipline and Punish: The Birth of the Prison*. Penguin.

2. Usher, R. & Edwards, R. [1994] *Postmodernism and Education*. Routledge, p. 96.

3. Lacan, J. [1949] 'The Mirror Stage as Formative of the Function of the I as Revealed in Psychoanalytic Experience' in Sheridan, A. (trans.) [1977] *Ecrits*. Routledge, pp. 17.

4. Ibid.

5. Lacan, J. [1977] op. cit., p. 303. For a brief description of this term see Evens, D. [1996] *An Introductory Dictionary of Lacanian Psychoanalysis*, p. 149. For a lengthy theoretical application of this term to ideological fields see, Zizek, S. [1989] *The Sublime Object of Ideology*, Verso.

6. Coward, R. & Ellis, J. [1977] *Language and Materialism*. Routledge & Kegan Paul.

7. Inner London Education Authority ILEA [1986] GCSE Art and Design: Video 1, Session: Differentiation, ILEA Learning Resources Branch, Television and Publishing Centre, London. Produced in collaboration with the University of London Schools Examinations Board and Norman Binch, ILEA Staff Inspector for Art and Design.

8. DFE (1995] *Art in the National Curriculum*. London: HMSO.

9. The School Curriculum and Assessment Authority [1996] *Consistency in Teacher Assessment: Exemplification of Standards*. London: SCAA.

10. Ibid. p. 9.

11. Copjec, J. [1995] *Read My Desire: Lacan Against the Historicists*. MIT Press, p. 34.

12. Burgin, V. [1987] *The End of Art Theory*. Macmillan, p. 41.

13. Read, H. [1944] *Education Through Art*. Faber & Faber.

14. The term difference is dealt with at length by Derrida [1967] *Speech and Phenomena and Other Essays on Husserl's Theory of Signs*, trans. David B. Allison, Northwestern University Press [1973]. For an accessible introduction to Derrida, see Collins, J. & Mayblin, W. [1996] *Derrida for Beginners*, Ikon Books, and Norris, C. [1987] *Derrida*. Fontana Press.

15. For theorizations of culture and identity, see Hall, S. & du Gay, P. (eds.) [1996] *Questions of Cultural Identity*. Sage; Bhabba, H. K. [1994] *The Location of Culture*, Routledge; and Woodward, K. (ed.) [1997] *Identity and Difference*. Sage/The Open University.

Originally published in the *Journal of Art & Design Education*, volume 18 (1) 1999.

Chapter 13: Assessment in Educational Practice: Forming Pedagogised Identities in the Art Curriculum

Dennis Atkinson

(Acknowledgement: Thanks to Carla Mindel and her students at Highgate Wood School, London)

Introduction: The Ambassadors

There is a painting by Holbein housed in the National Gallery in London entitled *The Ambassadors*, which has been employed by Lacan and others to illustrate their explorations of identity, representation and meaning. I want to use this picture to begin my study of the discourses in which teachers and students develop and acquire their pedagogised identities, that is to say their identities as learners and teachers. However I will provide my own interpretation of Holbein's painting to suit my purpose. The painting is well known. Two richly clothed dignitaries are standing either side of a set of shelves on which are displayed collections of objects and measuring instruments. They look out towards the viewer. In the central foreground, rising from the base, there is a mysterious form which appears as a smudge, a fuzzy image. If the viewer takes up a position to the extreme right of the painting the smudge is transformed and reveals itself to be a representation of a skull. The technical term for this visual manipulation or distortion of form is anamorphosis. It is a technique which interested painters of the period. The interesting point about the painting is that from a frontal perspective this meaningless shape is surrounded by meaning, that is to say, all around the mysterious shape meaning is abundant in the form of recognisable representations. This idea of lack at the centre of a field of meaning, this apparent void in the midst of recognisable form, is something I will explore in relation to assessment practices.

In school art lessons some students produce mysterious images which are difficult to interpret, they are rather like the meaningless smudge in Holbein's painting. That is to say, within the discourses through which we form understanding of representational practice and which constitute assessment criteria, these images are a mystery. But if we are able to change our perspective, if we are disturbed enough to reflect upon the hermeneutic structure of our interpretational discourse there is the possibility of forming a new hermeneutic, rather similar to taking up a different viewing position before Holbein's painting, so that meaning emerges. I shall discuss such disturbance leading to the possibility of a change in perspective in order to effect a more inclusive approach to assessment and, consequently, a radicalisation of perceptions of students as learners.

In this rather speculative paper my particular focus will be assessment in educational practices with specific focus upon assessing drawing from observation. In my experience assessing children's or student's art work has always been a problematic aspect of teaching art in schools. There are some who feel that to even consider assessing art work is rather pointless because art is concerned with self-expression and we should value equally each individual's form of expression and representation. Others feel that it is possible to assess student's art work if we select the appropriate criteria and forms of judgment. My purpose in this paper is to consider how assessment as a discursive practice can be considered as an apparatus of visibility and surveillance. I want to discuss how assessment in art practice actually constructs or makes visible both student's and teacher's pedagogised identities. To begin consider the five drawings below. They were produced in a lesson where the students (age 11–12 years) worked in pairs and took turns to make a line drawing of their partner. This is a common drawing exercise in schools in the United Kingdom.

Many drawings which students produce are assimilated or recognized within codes of representation through which they achieve meaning. This is not because the

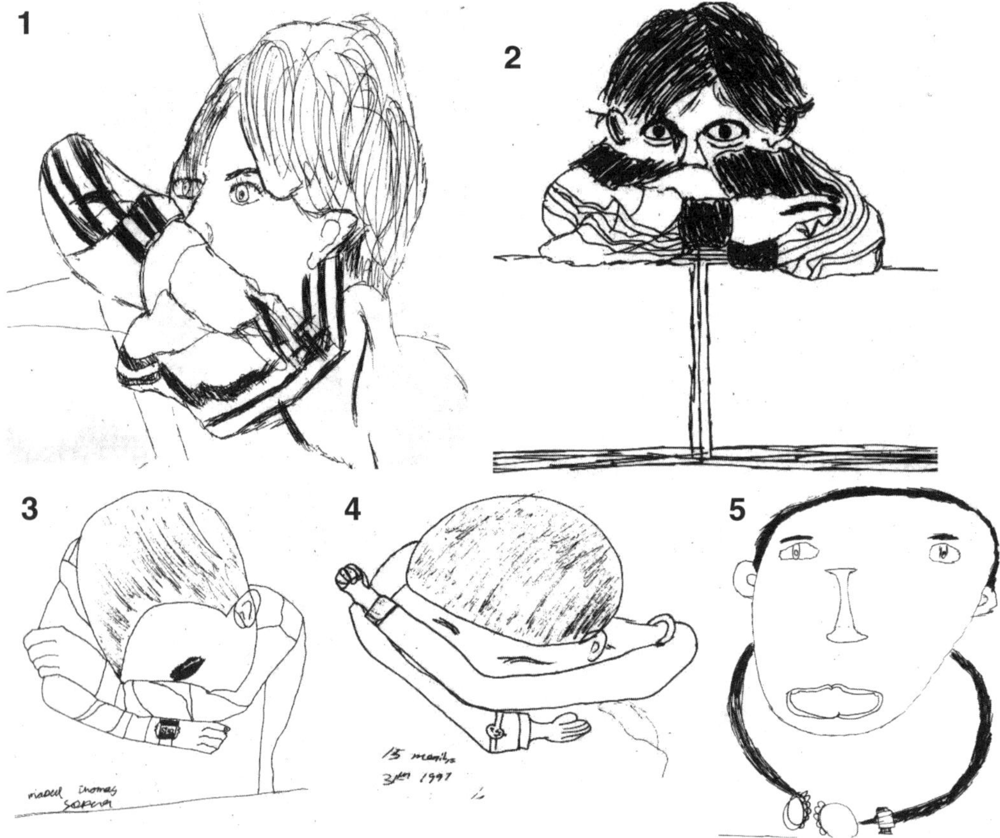

drawing reflects a visual correspondence with reality (although we might believe this to be the case) but because the drawing is recognized within accepted representational codes. However there are some drawings which jar, their form is mysterious and they are frequently regarded as poor representations which reflect a lack of drawing ability. The effect of the oddness or the singularity of such drawings upon a student's pedagogised identity is that the student frequently occupies a place of *otherness* in relation to the normative forms of accepted drawing practice. The student becomes what I call a *pedagogised other* of the accepted symbolic order of drawing practice. In Butler's terms, the student becomes a marginalized subject within the specific discourse in which drawing ability is assessed.

> *All identities operate through exclusion, through the discursive construction of a constitutive outside and the production of abjected and marginalised subjects, apparently outside the field of the symbolic, the representable, which then return to trouble and unsettle the foreclosures we call identities (my emphasis).[1]*

For me it is the drawing in Fig. 5, the one which troubles and unsettles my foreclosure, which I find interesting in relation to the task of assessment and the subsequent identification of the student as learner.

One possible scenario of assessment might be to regard drawings 1 and 2 as more effective representations than drawings 4 and 5 with drawing 3 lying somewhere between these pairings. Drawing 5 is strikingly different and could be regarded as weak or defective as a representational drawing. A poor representation which indicates that the student responsible for its production could be regarded as less able in drawing practice than the other students. In assessment discourse the drawings represent the subject of practice not simply for other subjects (teachers responsible for assessment) but primarily for other signifiers, that is to say, for the symbolic network of representational codes or discourses of visuality in which the drawings as signifiers have to be inserted to achieve meaning. We may acknowledge the representational forms of drawings 1 and 2 because they can be easily understood within accepted codes of representation. Equally we can marvel at the economy and sophistication of drawing 3, it is indeed a beautiful drawing in which the use of a mainly orthographic system produces a powerful representation of the solidity and positioning of the body. Drawings 4 and 5 in differing degrees disturb the representational codes we tend to employ when assessing such drawings. However, drawing 5 is so different, so singular, that it is not easily understood and it is likely to be assessed as weak or even child-like in relation to the other drawings. But if we regard this drawing as defective we also, by implication, construct its author's pedagogised identity accordingly. I shall argue there is another way of considering such strange drawings, but first I want to spend a little more time on assessment.

Assessment of student's art practices

There is a central difficulty embedded in the field of art in education. This relates to the difference between discursive frameworks within which we conceive and perceive art practice and the event or the act of practice. This difference mutates into that between a teacher's understanding of art practice gained from his or her work as an artist and the pedagogic requirement to initiate, understand and assess the art practices of students within the institution of art education. Frequently these differences are illustrated by many teachers' open acknowledgement *in theory* of the legitimacy of different ontological (ways of being) and epistemological (ways of knowing) orientations of individuals engaged in art practice and the teacher's imposition, *in practice*, of specific epistemological values which presuppose specific ontological orientations. Thus the outcomes of some practices and experiences are valued more than others. The imposition of value on students' art practices impacts upon the construction of both students' and teachers' pedagogised identities.

Consider the following statement from an assessment discourse about which I have written previously.[2] It is an assessment of student's painting of a building site:

> *Information about the shapes of buildings and machinery which feature in the environment has been observed and recorded but greater analysis is needed in order to represent this accurately.[3]*

The following statements are taken from a secondary school art department's assessment policy:

> *To be viewed excellent a student: can clearly visualize and record accurately using appropriate basic elements.*

Some assessment statements on individual students taken from their progress reports state:

> *A is able to record from observation from a wide range of sources with some accuracy.*
> *B is able to record accurately from observation.*
> *C has difficulty recording responses to observations … and needs to use imaging skills including scale, perspective and composition.*

The words *accurately* or *accuracy* suggest that representation is a matter of attempting to achieve a visual correspondence with viewed reality, the purpose of representation is to achieve optical truth. These terms are signifiers which, within the assessment discourse, presuppose a particular ontology and epistemology of visual experience in which the world can be perceived, understood and represented through the representational medium 'as it is.' Information from the world passes directly through the retinal membrane and is directly translated into a graphic form. It is the translation of this perceptual information into a graphic representation which is anticipated as a matter of drawing skill.

The signifier *accuracy* thus presupposes an objective world, which is knowable or perceivable as it is through representational form. This signifier provides the crucial semantic pivot around which meaning is structured in the assessment statements above. A student's pedagogised identity is constructed therefore according to the level of graphic skills which the representational form exhibits. The drawing system which is often viewed as facilitating optical truth is perspectival projection and it is this representational system which often forms the benchmark for determining the representational efficacy or accuracy of an observational drawing and consequently, in determining a student's pedagogised identity as a subject of drawing practice. Frequently this relationship is cemented by what Bryson[4] calls the *natural attitude* towards representation. Put simply this attitude assumes a visual correspondence between the form of objects in the world and the form of objects as represented on the drawing surface, when viewed from a particular position. In the drawings of children and students a drawing's representational form is often assessed according to its degree of natural correspondence with a particular view of the real object.

What I want to do next is to introduce a series of conceptual terms from the work of Jacques Lacan in order to try to theorise how assessment as a discursive practice produces pedagogised identities. I shall draw upon Zizek's interpretation and exposition of key Lacanian terms in order to develop a critical reading of common assumptions concerning the relationship between an observational drawing and its referent in the world.

It is with the notions of inclusion and exclusion in the construction of pedagogised identities as these are formed in assessment practices with which I am concerned. I shall argue that the natural attitude to representation consists of a fantasy which fetishises student's drawings and the notion of ability. That is to say that ability is viewed as being *in* the student and *in* the drawing. I will suggest that assessment of observational drawing does not involve comparing the drawing's representational efficacy with an 'actual' view of objects (although this often appears to be the case), but relies upon the fantasy of an objective world which is representable as it is. This is a further fetishistic practice which hides the subjective production of objectivity (see Zizek 1997 p. 97).

Consequently, in assessment practices there is nothing behind or prior to the drawing which is directly accessible (such as a real object) except representational fantasies, that is to say a consensual system of signifiers, which already precede and go beyond the drawing. For assessment discourses and practices to avoid being dominated by the natural attitude to representation I argue that it is important to try to pass through this particular representational fantasy in order to establish a more inclusive approach for responding to the semiotic differences of student's representational practices.

However, passing through this fantasy does not imply that a place of truth will be attained on the part of the interpreter, but rather a new hermeneutic state whose epistemological foreclosure will, ultimately, be subject to further deconstruction and illumination.

Lacanian terminology[5]

Objet petit a: this can be understood as an object which causes desire, an object which we seek but which we never attain. It is a fantasy object, something which has no existence in reality but which nevertheless structures desire. It can be conceived as a fantasy object which lies beyond symbolisation but around which symbolisation circles. Attempts to reveal the essence of *society*, *tradition*, *democracy*, *intelligence*, *ability*, in order to expose their hidden kernel of meaning, always in the end fail because such terms are constituted upon an essential lack which is masked by the term itself. Each term can be viewed as constituting a fantasy object, *objet petit a*. The current concern for *standards* is an interesting illustration of *objet petit a* functioning within the politics of educational policy. This term, as Williams[6] shows, when acting as a plural singular is frequently employed for suasive or consensual purposes. When considered closely, unless specific standards in the sense of an ordinary plural, are identified for specific areas of practice, the use of *standards* as a plural singular seems to refer to something universal and unquestionable. Indeed, as Williams tells us, it is difficult 'to disagree with some assertion of standards without appearing to disagree with the very idea of quality.' But the concern for standards in education does not signify an unchanging, universal and permanent referent, for as societies change so do values, and even within specific socio-historical periods there are radical disagreements about standards. Thus this popular term has no essential meaning but develops meaning within specific ideological discourses.

Signifiers such as *standards* and, as I shall show, *ability*, are not points of density of meaning, although this appears to be the case, rather they can be viewed as signifiers without essential signifieds. They are conceived and experienced as points of plenitude of meaning[7] but it could be argued they occupy a place of lack. Such signifiers constitute the Lacanian *objet petit a* in the sense that their apparent reference to specific signifieds is created through a fantasy (ideology) object of desire (the need to 'raise standards'). Another way of talking about this is to recognize the relative nature of such discourses within their specific social and historical contexts. In teaching and learning contexts the term *ability* is often used by teachers to identify students' levels of understanding and practice, as though the word signified some inherent property which a student possessed. But considered another way it refers to a particular kind of behaviour which is deemed acceptable or desirable within particular practices and ideologies of teaching and learning. Often in the field of art in education students who are considered to be able drawers are those able to draw in a particular way, or put differently, able to employ a particular representational system. Thus the term *ability* does not identify an essential property but a form of behaviour or practice that is valued within specific paradigms of teaching and learning.

The well-known anecdote recounting the meeting of Zeuxis and Parrahasios provides an illustration of *objet petit a* functioning in the act of interpreting a visual representation. Whilst Zeuxis produced an image of grapes which appeared to fool birds, he is similarly deceived by Parrahasios who has painted a veil on the wall. Zeuxis asks Parrahasios to show what he has painted behind the veil. The key point is that the very 'act of concealing deceives us precisely by pretending to conceal something,'[8] and it is this 'something behind,' this essence or inner substance, which we seek which constitutes objet petit a … because of course there is nothing behind the image, only ourselves, our projections. In the practice of assessing students' drawings it is often the case that we look beyond the drawing to a supposed reality in order to consider the drawing's representational efficacy.

Point de capiton: this term translated into English as 'quilting point' or 'anchoring point' refers literally to an upholstery button, a device which pins down the stuffing in upholstery work. Analogously Lacan uses the term to discuss how particular signifiers retroactively stitch the subject into the signifying chain. Zizek develops the notion of quilting with reference to the Althusserian idea of interpellation and shows how key signifiers interpolate or hail individuals into subject positions. He describes how meaning is structured through key nodal points[9] or signifiers which articulate the truth of a particular ideological discourse. For example, if discourse concerned with freedom is quilted through communism a particular structure of meaning will develop, relating to class struggle and so on. On the other hand, if this discourse is quilted through an idea of liberal democracy a different structure of meaning develops. Zizek[10] argues that, what is at stake in the ideological struggle is which of the nodal points, *points de capiton*, will totalize, the structure of meaning. The *point de capiton* is thus a signifier which, as a signifier, unifies a given field, constitutes its identity: it is, so to speak, the word which things themselves refer to recognise themselves in their unity.[11] The importance of this term for the constitution of subjectivity and identity is crucial because individuals are interpellated into subject positions through discourses whose structure of meaning is unified by *points de capiton*.

> *The* point de capiton *is the point through which the subject is sewn to the signifier, and at the same time the point which interpellates individual into subject by addressing it*

The words *accurately* or *accuracy* as used in the above assessment statements function as Lacanian *points de capiton*. Theorising the term *accuracy* as a Lacanian *point de capiton*, invokes the possibility of a different epistemology and ontology of assessment practice to that produced within the natural attitude to perception and representation. It revokes the natural attitude to assessment in which representation is understood as the direct retrieval of information from the world via the process of perception, and offers the possibility of understanding representation as a signifying practice which constructs rather than retrieves perception and reality. The term *accuracy* creates the illusion of a directly accessible world and the illusion of the representational system's ability to retrieve its truth. It is the Lacanian *objet petit a*, a desired object, which lies behind the signifier *accuracy*, not a directly accessible world but only the illusion of such a reality. The desire for representational accuracy, as manifested in the assessment statements above, is therefore driven by two fetishised illusions, one consisting of a belief in an objective world which we can know 'as it is' and the other in a belief in the efficacy of a representational form to make such knowledge available. To push this a little further, it can be argued therefore that the assessment statements are grounded in the fantasy of a directly accessible world and a fantasy of a representational system which can elicit optical truth. If this is the case, student's representational practices and their pedagogised identities as art practitioners are assessed not according to an objective external criterion, such as optical truth, but in Lacanian parlance, according to fantasy constructions (*points de capiton*) which revolve around *objet petit a*; not real objects but objects of desire.

The Real: *It is that which resists symbolisation absolutely.*[13] This is perhaps the most difficult Lacanian concept to describe because, put quite simply, the Real is that which resists or is beyond signification. Nevertheless it has important implications for interpreting phenomena in the context of educational practice and assessment leading to the subsequent formation of students' and teachers' pedagogised identities.

Lacan's use of the term Real fluctuates as it is employed in different ways in his writings in relation to the orders of the imaginary and the symbolic. The most uncomplicated sense of this term refers to brute existence, to a 'hard impenetrable kernel that resists symbolisation.'[14] For most of the time our experience is understood through language, visual codes and other social structures. But occasionally what we experience goes beyond the symbolic register as Miller states:

The Real is a shock of a contingent encounter which disrupts the automatic circulation of the symbolic mechanism; a grain of sand preventing its smooth functioning; a traumatic encounter which ruins the balance of the symbolic universe of the subject.[15]

Bowie also describes the distinction between the Real and the symbolic:

The network of signifiers in which we have our being is not all that there is, and the rest of what is may chance to break in upon us at any moment.[16]

It is 'the rest of what is' which could be said to constitute the Lacanian Real and which we experience purely as contingent encounters which disrupt our symbolic frameworks. On encountering the Real, Bowie[17] argues that, 'the mind makes contact with the limits of its power, with that which its structure cannot structure.' This is an important factor to bear in mind when reflecting upon assessment practices in education.

The eruption of the Real within the symbolic order creates a destabilisation of our frameworks of understanding, this is the essential point. Peter Weir's film, *The Truman Show*, provides a beautiful illustration of this process. Truman's life (unknown to Truman) is totally constructed by a media mogul, Christo. All the people in Truman's world are actors who play his friends, business colleagues, even his wife. His entire life is lived within a gigantic film set. However during the film incidents occur, like the crashing to earth of a large spotlight, which Truman finds totally bewildering, they puncture his understanding and create instability within the symbolic order of his existence.

The Real then is that which cannot be accounted for within the symbolic universe, which, when it is encountered, cannot be understood. Although I have spoken of the Real as a disturbance of the symbolic, it is important not to forget that the symbolic order introduces a cut in the Real.[18] The Real is always primary, always there, but is largely overwhelmed by our ideas of reality which are the products of symbolisation. Lacan hints at the difference between reality and the Real:

It is the world of words which creates the world of things – things originally confused in the hic et nunc *of the all in the process of coming-into-being.[19]*

Thus as well as denoting that which lies beyond symbolisation, the Real, by implication, refers to that which is lacking in the symbolic order, a foreclosed element, that which is foreclosed by the symbolic and which can never be grasped.

But why is the Real relevant to this paper? Zizek[20] discusses the Real-as-object when describing writing not as signifier but simply as object. Drawing number 5 above could be regarded as a Real object, as something lying beyond our conventional frameworks of understanding. Such drawings disturb the ways in which we understand representation in drawing practice, they puncture the accepted representational codes.

Consequently we may need to consider and evaluate, not the drawing, but the very discourses and classification systems in which we understand and assess such drawings and student's art practices. We must, as Wittgenstein wrote in his *Remarks on Frazer's Golden Bough*, 'face the error and recognize the truth in it.' This may involve reflecting upon the epistemological frameworks which constitute our understanding and the ontology of a student's drawing practice. Such reflection may present us with possibilities for developing a more inclusive approach to the difference of students' art practices. Such reflections thus disrupt the power-knowledge frameworks of assessment in which student's pedagogised identities are forged and teacher's assessment practices are confirmed.

To return to drawing 5, this can be viewed rather like the smudge in Holbein's *Ambassadors*, in that it appears as a meaningless form in the midst of the discourses in which we understand representational form. Such drawings are, to quote Bryson,[21] 'so generically unplaceable,' however, rather than pathologise the image, we may gain more insight by assessing the lack in our understanding and moving towards a new discursive position, a realignment of discourse and image. This would entail a radical overhaul of the purpose of assessment in art in education and subsequently the way in which we understand student's art practices. The consequence of this may lead to what Grossberg[22] identifies as a 'project of constructing a form of knowledge which respects the other without absorbing it into the same ...' The difficulty, as Lacan reminds us, is that:

> *The signifier producing itself in the field of the Other, makes manifest the subject of its signification. But it functions as a signifier only to reduce the subject in question to being no more than a signifier, to petrify the subject in the same movement in which it calls the subject to function, to speak, as subject.*[23]

Concluding remarks

In this study I have focussed on the difficult practice of assessment. My intention is to expose what might be considered a cultural politics of representation in order to disturb specific assessment discourses in art education which constitute pedagogised identities. I have argued that the construction of pedagogised identity in observational drawing practices is not founded on assessing a student's ability to perceive and represent the world 'as it is.' Rather, such identity is constructed within specific discourses and representational codes which appear 'natural.'

I have argued that particular discursive terms e.g., *accuracy*, which appear to presuppose an objective world which is accessible through perceptual experience and reproduced in drawing, actually presuppose fantasy objects, *objets petit a*. I have also shown how assessment discourse fetishises ability as existing *in* the student or *in* the drawing. Consequently the constructive power of the discourse to produce pedagogised identities goes unnoticed and ability is taken to be a natural capacity. In disrupting the fantasy screen of assessment discourse, the Real-as-object reveals the lack in the discourse and, for a moment, can shift our gaze towards a greater accommodation of the difference of students' art practices.

Perhaps a way forward, as far as the art curriculum is concerned, is to acknowledge the need for order, as constituted by assessment practices, but to strive for a different kind of order. An order whose temporality is heterogeneous, an order which is grounded in a project of difference, an order which values different ontologies of practice, an order where the singular is not reduced to the normative, an order which is grounded in local experience.

Notes and References

1. Butler, J. [1993] *Bodies That Matter*. London: Routledge, p. 22.

2. Atkinson, D. [1999] 'A Critical Reading of the National Curriculum for Art in the Light of Contemporary Theories of Subjectivity,' *Journal of Art and Design Education*, vol. 18 no.1.

3. SCAA (1996) *Consistency in Teacher assessment: Exemplification of Standards*. Hayes, Middlesex: School Curriculum and Assesment Authority.

4. Bryson, N. [1983] *Vision and Painting: The logic of the gaze*. London: Macmillan, pp. 10–11. Bryson provides five principles which for him constitute the natural attitude to visual representation. Drawing extensively on his text I will provide a summary of four of these. 1. An absence of history. The basic visual field is consistent across generations and corresponds to the fixed nature of the optical body. Visual experience is thus universal and transhistorical and it is therefore possible to judge along a sliding scale how closely an image approximates the truth of perception. 2. Dualism. The retinal membrane separates the world of the mind from the world of extension. Outside a pre-existent reality flooded with light which is thus reflected inside by a passive specular consciousness. The self is not responsible for constructing the content of consciousness which is formed by the incoming stream of information from outside. 3. The centrality of perception. The natural attitude is unable to account for images which depart from universal visual experience except in negative terms: the painter has misperceived the optical truth or has been able through lack of skill to provide optical truth. 4. Communication. The representational image transports as perfectly as it can to the viewer the artists original perceptual experience.

5. The Lacanian terms I use in this paper arise frequently in Jacques Lacan's text, *Ecrits: A Selection*. A very accessible introduction to these terms can be found in Slavoj Zizek's book, *Looking Awry: An Introduction to Jacques Lacan Through Popular Culture* [1991] Cambridge Mass. London: MIT Press.

6. Williams, R. [1980] *Keywords*. London: Fontana/Croom Helm, p. 249.

7. Zizek, S. [1989] *The Sublime Object of Ideology*. London & New York: Verso, p. 99.

8. Ibid. p. 196.

9. Ibid. p. 87.

10. Ibid. p. 88.

11. Ibid. pp. 95–96.

12. Ibid. p. 101.

13. Lacan, J. [1988] *The Seminar. Book 1. Freud's Papers on Technique, 1953–54*, trans. J. Forrester, New York: Norton: Cambridge: Cambridge University Press, p. 66.

14. Ibid. p. 169.

15. Ibid. p. 13.

16. Bowie, D. [1991] *Lacan*. London: Fontana, p. 103.

17. Ibid. p. 105.

18. See Evans, D. [1996] *An Introductory Dictionary of Lacanian Psychoanalysis*. London & New York: Routledge, p. 159.

19. Lacing, J. [1977] *Ecrits, A Selection*, trans. Alan Sheridan, London: Routledge, p. 65.

20. Ibid. p. 171.

21. Ibid. p. 187.

22. Grossberg, L. [1996] 'Identity and Cultural Studies – Is That All there Is?' in Hall, S. & du Gay, S. *Questions of Cultural Identity*. London: Sage, p. 103.

23. Lacan, J. [1986] *Four Fundamental Concepts of Psychoanalysis*, trans. Alan Sheridan. London: Penguin. p. 207.

Originally published in the *Journal of Art & Design Education*, volume 20 (1) 2001.

Notes on Contributors

Nicholas Addison is a lecturer in Art, Design & Museology, School of Arts & Humanities at the Institute of Education, University of London and teaches on the PGCE, MA, EdD and Ph.D. courses: he is course leader for the MA Art & Design in Education. For sixteen years he taught art and design and art history at a comprehensive school and a sixth form college in London. He has lectured in art history on BA courses and was chair of the Association of Art Historians Schools Group (1998–2003). He co-edited with Burgess, L. *Learning to Teach Art & Design in the Secondary School* (2000) and *Issues in Art & Design Teaching* (2003) both published by Routledge Falmer. His research interests include: critical studies, intercultural education, sexualities and identity politics. He has recently directed an AHRB funded research project, *Art Critics and Art Historians in Schools*.

Dennis Atkinson (Ph.D.) is Reader at Goldsmiths College, University of London and head of the MPhil/Ph.D. Programme in the Department of Educational Studies. He taught for seventeen years in secondary school and was head of art for twelve years. He gained his Ph.D. from the University of Southampton in 1988. He was the course leader for the PGCE Art and Design Secondary Course at Goldsmiths for ten years and still contributes to this programme. He is MA tutor for modules in *Visual Culture and Education, Culture, Pedagogy and Curriculum*, and *Contemporary Art, Identity and Education* which is taught in association with Tate Modern in London. His research interests include art and design in education and initial teacher education. He has a particular interest in employing hermeneutic, post-structural and psychoanalytic theory to explore the formation of pedagogised identities and practices within educational contexts. He is currently Principal Editor of *The International Journal of Art and Design Education* and has published regularly in academic journals since 1991. He has published two books, *Art in Education: Identity and Practice*, (Kluwer Academic Publishers) and an edited volume with Paul Dash, *Social and Critical Practice in Art Education* (Trentham Books).

Lesley Burgess is a Lecturer in Art and Design Education at the Institute of Education, London. The focus of her current research is The Value of Contemporary Art and Artists in Education.

John Danvers is an artist, writer and educator. He has exhibited widely in the UK, Canada, USA and Australia, and made presentations at many conferences around the world. John is currently working on a book for Rodopi about art, poetry and consciousness (due for publication spring 2006).

'Over the past few years I've been making drawings, texts and mixed-media presentations that are enactments of, and enquiries into, consciousness and mind. I've been trying to construct, and give form to, a metaphysics of indeterminacy and

awakening through multi-linear visual and textual narratives and notations. My research also involves the development of a radical pedagogy for art based on a belief in art as a philosophical practice, a mode of metaphysical enquiry.'

John is based at the University of Plymouth where he is Deputy Head of the School of Art & Performance and a Teaching Fellow of the university.
Website: www.johndanversart.co.uk

Paul Duncum is Associate Professor at The School of Art and Design of The University of Illinois at Urbana-Champaign. A former graphic designer and art and design high school teacher, in 1991 he received the Manuel Barkan Memorial Award for scholarship. As a long-time proponent of studying popular culture as part of art education, he has extensively published on issues relating popular culture to art education. He has employed a number of concepts to do this, including dominant culture, new times, everyday aesthetics, an aesthetic of embodiment, globalisation and visual culture. The latter includes the 2001 book he co-edited, *On Knowing: Art and Visual Culture*, published by Canterbury Press and the upcoming anthology he is editing, *Visual Culture in the Classroom: Case studies* to be published by the National Art Education Association. Critical Theory and Cultural Studies inform his work.

Lee Emery (Ph.D.) is Associate Professor in Arts Education at The University of Melbourne, Australia. She spent four months study leave at the University of Surrey, Roehampton in London during 2000 at which time she interviewed secondary art teachers in England. She has been a past editor of Australian Art Education and has been awarded an honorary life membership of the Australian Institute of Art Education. She was co-author of the National Statement and Profiles for Australian schools and has contributed to subsequent curriculum development in Victorian schools. She has also co-authored a book entitled *Effective Assessment of the Visual Arts* (Longman) and is currently preparing a text on the teaching of contemporary art in secondary schools.

Tom Hardy has worked as an art teacher in secondary schools for 23 years and has led art departments in inner-city, mixed, single sex and selective schools. He sat on the editorial board of *The International Journal of Art and Design Education* for eight years and acted as reviews editor for four. He is also a frequent contributor to other publications on art educational matters.

Stuart MacDonald studied fine art at Grays School of Art, Aberdeen, and later completed a Ph.D. at the Architecture School of the University of Liverpool. He is Director of the Lighthouse, which is Scotland's National Centre for Architecture, Design and is central to the promotion of Scotland's architecture policy and is the country's lead body on design. Previously, he worked for Glasgow 1999 UK City of

Architecture and Design and Glasgow's 1996 International Design Festival. He was a member of the recent Ministerial working group on the Creative Industries in Scotland. He was editor of the recently published *Scottish Architecture 2000–2002*. He is currently an external examiner at the University of Dundee and recently was made an Honorary Fellow of the Royal Institute of British Architects.

Sarat Maharaj is currently Professor of Visual Art and Knowledge Systems, Lund University. He was the first Rudolf Arnheim Professor at Humboldt University, Berlin (2000–01) and co-curator of *Documenta X1* 2002. His recent research and publications cover cultural translation and difference and visual art as knowledge production.

Robin Marriner is a senior lecturer in Visual Culture at Bath Spa University. He teaches theory and recent art history to, for the most part, art and design students. For its lifespan from 1990 to 2004, he taught on, and was course director for, the MA Visual Culture at Bath. He has published on aspects of contemporary art in various British art journals, wrote the essay on Derrida in *A Companion to Art Theory* (Blackwells) and presently has *Paying One's Dues: refiguring agency, authenticity and originality* and *The Photography of Frank, Friedlander and The Aesthetics of Abstract Painting* in preparation.

Malcolm Miles (Ph.D.) is Reader in Cultural Theory at the University of Plymouth, and author of *Art, Space & the City* (1997) and *Urban Avant-Gardes* (2004). He is co-Editor of *The City Cultures Reader* (2nd revised edition 2003) and *Urban Futures* (2003), and co-author of *The Consuming City* (2004).

Diane Reay is Professor of Sociology at the University of North London. She has worked extensively with Bourdieu's social theory and is particularly interested in feminist interventions in relation to social class.

John Steers (Ph.D.) was appointed General Secretary of the National Society for Art Education (now the National Society for Education in Art and Design) in 1981 after fourteen years teaching art and design in secondary schools in London and Bristol. He was the 1993–96 President of the International Society for Education through Art and served on its executive committee in several capacities between 1983 and the present. He has served on many national committees and as a consultant to government agencies. He has published widely on curriculum, assessment and policy issues. He is a trustee of the Higher Education in Art and Design Trust and the Chair of the Trustees of the National Arts Education Archive, University of Leeds. He is also a visiting Senior Research Fellow at Roehampton University, London.

John Swift (Ph.D.) is Emeritus Professor of Art Education University of Central England in Birmingham. Until his retirement from UCE in 2001 he was Professor of Art Education, Director of Studies Art Education, Chief Editor of ARTicle Press, Principal Editor of the *Journal of Art & Design Education* for the National Society of Education in Art & Design, MA Art & Education Course Director and Keeper of Archives. His interest in the history, theory and practice of art education is evident in many publications and conferences both here and abroad, and in his supervision of masters and doctoral students. Since retirement to south-west Scotland he has written *An Illustrated History of Moseley School of Art: Art Education in Birmingham 1800–1975*, and, with his wife, begun a local publishing house, 'an machair press,' and opened a gallery showing their respective work. Contact via jacquie.swift@virgin.net